SCHOOL, FAMILY, AND COMMUNITY

Techniques and Models for Successful Collaboration

Michael J. Dietz, PhD, Editor
Principal
Lake Shore Middle School
Mequon-Thiensville School District
Mequon, Wisconsin

with
Jamie Whaley
Editor, Aspen Publishers, Inc.

AN ASPEN PUBLICATION®
Aspen Publishers, Inc.
Gaithersburg, Maryland
1997

Library of Congress Cataloging-in-Publication Data

Dietz, Michael J.
School, family, and community : techniques and
models for successful collaboration / Michael J. Dietz.
p. cm.
Includes bibliographical references.
ISBN 0-8342-0708-7
1. Home and school—United States.
2. Education—Parent participation—United States.
3. Community and school—United States. I. Title.
LC225.3.D54 1997
306.43—dc21
97-42
CIP

Aspen Publishers, Inc., grants permission for photocopying for limited personal or internal use.
This consent does not extend to other kinds of copying, such as copying for general distribution,
for advertising or promotional purposes, for creating new collective works, or for resale.
For information, address Aspen Publishers, Inc., Permissions Department,
200 Orchard Ridge Drive, Suite 200, Gaithersburg, Maryland 20878.

Orders: (800) 638-8437
Customer Service: (800) 234-1660

About Aspen Publishers • For more than 35 years, Aspen has been a leading professional
publisher in a variety of disciplines. Aspen's vast information resources are available in both
print and electronic formats. We are committed to providing the highest quality information
available in the most appropriate format for our customers. Visit Aspen's Internet site for more
information resources, directories, articles, and a searchable version of Aspen's full catalog,
including the most recent publications: **http://www.aspenpub.com**
Aspen Publishers, Inc. • The hallmark of quality in publishing
Member of the worldwide Wolters Kluwer group.

Editorial Resources: Ruth Bloom
Library of Congress Catalog Card Number: 97-42
ISBN: 0-8342-0708-7

Printed in the United States of America

1 2 3 4 5

Contents

Foreword

Across the country, many educators, parents, community members, and students are seeking ideas and advice to achieve the goal of improving school, family, and community partnerships. This book is chock full of good ideas and examples of workable, useful practices to meet that goal.

The chapters in this volume are arranged to help readers learn about the framework of six types of involvement that create a comprehensive program.[1] The types of involvement—*Type 1*–Parenting, *Type 2*–Communicating, *Type 3*–Volunteering, *Type 4*–Learning at Home, *Type 5*–Decision Making, and *Type 6*–Collaborating with Community—may be activated by hundreds of practices. But which ones are feasible? Each chapter presents activities that have been designed and implemented by school, district, and state leaders and parents from many parts of the United States who have been working to improve their partnership programs. These are real, practical actions that can be adopted for use in elementary, middle, and high schools in urban, suburban, and rural communities.

Several chapters are particularly full. Chapter 2 includes many *Type 1* examples that meet "challenges" for partnerships to succeed. These include conducting some workshops for parents away from school in communities where families live, and designing ways to assist and involve families who do not always feel welcome at school, such as homeless parents, those who speak a language other than English,

and those who may not be able to travel easily to school. Chapter 3 provides many *Type 2* examples and discussions on parent-teacher conferences and newsletters, and looks into the World Wide Web as a new tool for home-school communications. Chapter 4 offers *Type 3* ideas and forms for recruiting and deploying volunteers effectively. Chapter 7 offers numerous *Type 6* activities that connect schools and families with their communities in ways that benefit students and families in productive business partnerships, timely health services, and other community programs and activities.

Why should schools and families work together to create comprehensive programs of partnerships? Isn't any *one* type of involvement enough? Studies show that the six types of involvement are represented by different practices, set different challenges for excellence, and yield different results. That is, not all practices to involve families lead quickly or directly to student learning or higher test scores. For example, some practices are more likely to increase *parents'* confidence such as *Type 1* workshops for parents and family resource centers. Other practices are more likely to increase *students'* skills, such as *Type 3* volunteers who work with children on reading, or *Type 4* interactive homework that engages students and families in conversations about math or other subjects. By understanding the types of involvement, their challenges, and likely results, educators and families will be better able to purposely select practices to meet specific goals for students, families, and schools.

Readers who find this book useful may be ready to take the next step to obtain assistance by joining the National Network of Partnership-2000 Schools at Johns Hopkins University.[2] In this network, schools, districts, and states are guided to use an Action Team approach to take stock of present practices of partnerships (as suggested in Chapter 1 of this volume) and to plan programs and practices using the framework of six types of involvement (as outlined in Chapters 2-7 of this volume). This work can, of course, be conducted independently, but the Network provides materials, guidance, and opportunities to share good ideas and solve problems through interactions with re-searchers and other schools, districts, and states working on the same issues.

Dr. Dietz, a talented school administrator, has a deep understanding of the nature of school, family, and community partnerships at all school levels. His timely collection and thoughtful comments should help many readers see that it is important and *possible* to develop and maintain responsive programs of school, family, and community partnerships. It is time to meet this goal!

Joyce L. Epstein, PhD
Director, Center for School, Family and
Community Partnerships
Johns Hopkins University
Baltimore, Maryland

REFERENCES

1. J.L. Epstein, School/Family/Community Partnerships: Caring for the Children We Share, *Phi Delta Kappan*, 76 (1995): 701–712.

2. J.L. Epstein, L. Coates, K.C. Salinas, M.G. Sanders, and B.S. Simon (in press, 1977). *School, Family, and Community Partnerships: Your Handbook for Action.* Thousand Oaks, CA: Corwin Press.

Introduction

PURPOSE OF THIS RESOURCE

These are exciting and challenging times for school leaders throughout the Untied States. Daily, superintendents, principals, and others responsible for developing effective, high-quality educational programs within districts and schools feel and respond to community pressure on many issues. This publication is a response to a growing need of practitioners in the field to have an effective resource for developing proactive practices that promote positive parent, family, and community relationships with schools. Each chapter of *School, Family, and Community* provides active, entrepreneurial school leaders with proven practices that will enhance the quality and effectiveness of parent, family, and community involvement in ways that benefit learning outcomes for children.

WORLD CLASS SCHOOLS

Creating "world class" schools requires devotion to developing programs valued by the community for their quality teaching and learning outcomes for children. In addition, world class schools seek to include families and communities in ways that promote and "tell the story" of the schools and the district. The relentless pressure placed on us as school leaders at all levels makes it critical that we proactively promote the goodness and excellence of our efforts for children. The school and district leaders of today must envision a future with richer partnerships between schools and both the families and communities that they serve.

THE SIX-TYPE MODEL

The strategies proposed in *School, Family, and Community* are based on a renowned model of parent and family involvement developed by Dr. Joyce Epstein, a researcher at Johns Hopkins University in Baltimore. This model is nonhierarchical—none of the six types of methods to promote involvement has higher priority than any other. Each of the six types has specific characteristics.

- **Type 1** relates to the basic obligation of parents and the ways in which schools can help them to develop parenting skills (Chapter 2).
- **Type 2** involves the basic obligations of schools and districts to develop both one-way and two-way communications with families and the community (Chapter 3).
- **Type 3** focuses on developing quality school volunteer practices (Chapter 4).
- **Type 4** stresses ways for schools to show parents and families how to help children with schoolwork (Chapter 5).
- **Type 5** examines the emerging role of parents in the decision making of school leaders (Chapter 6).
- **Type 6** emphasizes the importance of developing strong, effective links

between the school and the community (Chapter 7).

Based on more than a decade of research, this model is coherent, valid, and reliable. The intuitive, common sense approach in use of the model is helpful to school staffs, families, and community members in efforts to develop quality practices that will foster mutual involvement.

HOW TO USE THIS BOOK

This book is designed to reward browsing in any direction. Jump in where you feel engaged.

Chapters 1–6 provide a comprehensive look at promoting and developing both school and district relationships with the parents and the community. Sample assessment tools presented in Chapter 1 provide a means for school leaders to determine strengths and targets for growth in developing relationships with the school community. The first five types of Epstein's model, presented in Chapters 2–6, provide a foundation for the use of assessment data and information given in those chapters.

Chapter 7 focuses on creating and maintaining high-quality partnerships between schools and the communities they serve. To achieve the ambitious Goals 2000 and Workforce 2000 goals, school leaders must engage the entire community. If it takes an entire community to raise a child, it certainly requires all sectors of every community to contribute to school improvement. The models and samples of collaborative partnerships contained in Chapter 7 provide educational leaders with effective, adaptable tools for bringing schools and communities together for children. In an environment of limited resources, school leaders must explore the potential that quality relationships may provide as a way to both secure and further quality education for children.

CHANGING WITH THE TIMES

Are you prepared with the skills necessary to create and nurture parent, family, and community involvement practices as we move toward the twenty-first century? This may mean rethinking your role in working with the entire school community. Today's parents and community members expect school leaders to listen to them and to include them in new and meaningful ways. The successful school leaders of the future will respond to this challenge with vigor.

WHY BOTHER?

Why commit to broadening the scope and increasing the intensity of efforts with parents, families, and the community? These changing times require emphasis on academic achievement and caring for children at all levels of our district and school operations. Borrowing from the popular leadership literature, consider Tom Peters' challenge to organizations of the 1990s to "fascinate, bewitch, dazzle, and delight" their customers. As you move your schools into the twenty-first century, do you know and understand the school community that you lead and serve? Believe it or not, school choice is alive and well in the majority of communities, but most of us still believe that if we simply open our doors the children will come. Think again!

Getting the most out of materials contained in this resource requires deep involvement with the concept of parent, family, and community. It is impossible to become deeply involved in this work and emerge unchanged. Through your efforts and the efforts of those around you, relationships throughout the school community will take on a different perspective. In meeting the challenge to develop world class schools, you will forge stronger relationships with staff, parents, families, community, and most importantly, the students you serve.

Michael J. Dietz, PhD

CHAPTER 1

Evaluating and Improving Programs and Participation Rates

Before new parent and community programs are established, current programs should be reviewed and attempts should be made to determine why people do not participate in them. This process can be used to identify weaknesses in existing practices, to develop ideas for programs that would meet the needs of parents dissatisfied with current programs, and to prevent administrators from repeating mistakes that lead to lack of involvement.

TYPES OF ASSESSMENT

Assessments should take place both internally and externally. In the internal assessment, principals or site administrators should complete a self-analysis of the number and types of opportunities offered for parent and community involvement. In the external assessment, parents and community members should be questioned about how they perceive the school's communications, involvement opportunities, cooperativeness, and overall atmosphere.

Internal Assessment

Some survey tools used by education researchers to assess the degree of parent involvement in schools may also be used as self-inventories to measure the individual school's responsiveness to parent needs and its degree of community participation. Resource 1–1 is a portion of a survey developed by Michael Dietz, PhD, principal at Lake Shore Middle School in Mequon, Wisconsin. The survey was used to study parent involvement in the state's middle schools. Individual administrators can use the same form to evaluate a school's strengths and weaknesses simply by completing it and reviewing their responses. A second evaluation tool is a checklist developed by the Families in Education Program of the Wisconsin Department of Public Instruction (Resource 1–2). This checklist can also be used to measure how actively administrators involve parents, families, and community members in schools. The list includes statements related to all six of Dr. Joyce Epstein's involvement categories (parenting and family skills, communication, learning at home, volunteering, governance and advocacy, and community outreach). For example, the statement, "We have a structured program to help parents assist their children with homework," is included under "Learning at Home." A principal checks the boxes next to those statements that apply and can then easily determine the areas in which the school must improve.

However, Dietz reminds administrators that, during the internal assessment, both program depth and program participation must be considered. A school may use 20 different outreach methods, he says, but if only a fraction of the target audience participates in those programs, the school neither truly involves parents and community residents nor realizes the benefits of successful programs.

Individual programs should be assessed, too, says Mercedes Fitzmaurice, senior research specialist at Research for Better Schools, in Philadelphia, Pennsylvania. A decision-making table (Resource 1–3) developed by her agency helps school leaders evaluate programs on the basis of educational benefits to students, external benefits to students, benefits to parents and community residents, benefits to school staff and faculty, cost, and potential economic impact on the community at large. This table was developed primarily for small, rural schools with limited resources, to help them assess which programs would provide maximum benefit to students and the overall community. However, the same criteria can be applied to larger schools, many of which are in urban areas, where resources are limited and community return is important.

A unique feature of the table allows schools and districts to weight specific categories and questions according to local priorities. School leaders can assess programs on the basis of the needs of the school and community situations, rather than predetermined research criteria. Fitzmaurice recommends that small groups of school staff and community stakeholders work together to complete the table as a way to build consensus about the future of programs and proposals.

Other researchers have also developed evaluation tools. Epstein encourages school leaders to answer the nine questions in Exhibit 1–1. These questions are designed for use in assessing the success of school, family, and community partnerships and programs. They can help school leaders to determine how to improve existing programs and meet needs not addressed by those programs. The questions address

the degree of investment that school personnel must make. They also quiz administrators on follow-through issues, such as "How will you evaluate the results of your efforts?"

External Assessment

The purpose of outreach programs is to meet community needs and reflect residents' opinions on school issues. Consequently, identification of these needs and opinions is essential to the assessment process. One approach is to invite community stakeholders who are not part of the school community to complete the decision-making table (Resource 1–3). More pointed assessments may be needed, however, when programs involve a specific group of people, such as parents. Specific opinions should be gathered from a target audience by use of a telephone or direct mail survey.

All assessment procedures should be ongoing to monitor changes in community and parent needs and to ensure growth and success.

REASONS FOR LACK OF INVOLVEMENT

Key questions to be asked during the assessment phase are, "Why don't people become involved in school activities?" and "Do we, as school leaders, make everyone feel welcome?" Understanding the answers to these questions is essential to improving program participation rates. "You have to find [individuals'] involvement pressure points and address them," says Dietz.

Frequently, he says, people avoid schools because they do not feel comfortable there. Brown[1] notes Greenberg's finding[2] that many uninvolved parents feel unable to become involved in school activities because of their own negative experiences as

Exhibit 1–1   Epstein's Nine Questions To Identify Success

1. Which partnership practices are currently working well at each grade level?
2. Which partnership practices should be improved or added in each grade?
3. How do you want your school's family involvement practices to look 3 years from now?
4. Which present practices should change and which should continue?
5. Which families are you reaching, and which are hard to reach?
6. What can be done better to communicate with the latter?
7. What costs are associated with the improvements you want?
8. How will you evaluate the results of your efforts?
9. What opportunities will you arrange for teachers, parents, and students to share?

Source: Reprinted with permission from Dietz, M.J. (1992), Principals and Parent Involvement in Wisconsin Middle Level Public Schools. Ph.D. Dissertation, in Madison, WI, University of Wisconsin.

students or because of differences between their cultural styles and/or socioeconomic levels and those of teachers. Other factors may also contribute to low participation rates.

Quality of Relationships with School Staff

Individuals relate to school personnel who listen and respond to their concerns. As a result, they are more likely to become involved in school activities. Swick[3] says findings by Comer and Haynes[4] suggest that when parents sense an inviting school climate, they are more supportive of teachers, and parent participation in school activities increases.

Several researchers have identified qualities that promote strong relationships between parents and teachers. Comer and Haynes say the teacher qualities that appeal most to parents are trust, warmth, closeness, positive self-image, effective classroom management, child-centeredness, positive discipline, nurturance, and effective teaching skills. Characteristics that influence relationships in general are warmth, openness, sensitivity, flexibility, reliability, and accessibility.

Likewise, Epstein[5] and Galinsky[6] found that the following teacher attributes are related to highly successful parent involvement: positive attitudes, active planning to involve parents, continuous teacher training, involvement in professional growth, and personal competence.

Internal assessments should examine these elements and identify all avenues for improvement.

Differences in Language and Culture

Schools and their neighborhoods are increasingly diverse, and it is imperative that administrators be attuned to cultural differences in all facets of education, including communication, partnerships, programs, and general administration. Recognizing and accommodating differences in these areas create a more inviting atmosphere for members of all cultures and often generate greater participation in school activities.

Attention to cultural differences also can pay dividends in attempts (1) to understand why parents do not participate and (2) to develop strategies to reverse that trend. Nicolau and Ramos,[7] for example, have found that Mexican-American parents see the school's role as instilling knowledge and the parents' role as providing for basic needs and teaching respect and proper behavior. They note that the two roles should not interfere with each other. After examining 42 projects to foster involvement, the researchers concluded that the following strategies can be used to improve a school's relationship with these parents: reception areas that include bilingual staff; telephone calls and written communication in Spanish, as well as English; and personal visits at a neutral site, such as a community center, rather than at school or in the home.[8]

Additional points to be conscious of when interacting with people of other cultures are the need to allow personal space and sufficient time for response to questions, the importance of eye contact, and the significance of touching.

Inappropriate Assignments and Feedback to Volunteers

Dietz says that administrators can benefit from applying the rule of "different strokes for different folks" to parents and community residents who volunteer to help with school projects. "It's a matter of applying principles of the *One-Minute Manager*[9] and giving people what they need."

If individuals are willing and able to take on responsibility, they should be given responsibility. If volunteers are not comfortable in the school environment, the teacher should begin with short-term, manageable tasks that require no background in education and minimal decision making. This approach addresses common fears of would-be volunteers—that they will be assigned projects for which they feel completely unqualified or, conversely, that they will be given monotonous tasks that do not capitalize on their talent and experience.

MEASURES TO IMPROVE PARTICIPATION

Implementation of Policies To Promote Parent Participation

Schools that regularly invite parents to participate in activities and attend school functions should have in place a policy approved by the school board. This measure is especially important for schools that require or are considering a requirement that parents participate in a minimum number of school activities each year.

A family involvement policy document should begin with a statement of the school's desire for parent involvement. The policy should specify the degree of involvement expected and should give nuts-and-bolts information about how parents can become more active in school activities. Conversely, policies may also limit the extent to which parents may become involved. A policy may state that parents can participate on building committees and have input on site decisions, for example, but that they cannot vote on school governance issues, or vice versa.

In development of a family involvement policy, special attention should be paid to the policy's title. The goal is involvement regardless of the name of the policy, but it is important to show sensitivity to the fact that not all students live with their parents and that not all parents come in pairs. The policy should use language that openly invites all people who care for students to participate in school activities and should not cause a nonparent guardian to feel that he or she will not fit in or be welcome.

Three sample family-involvement policies are shown in Resource 1–4. The first policy takes a top-down approach, stating obligations of the school board. The second policy addresses obligations of all parties involved, including school personnel and families. This policy also refers to parent volunteer requirements. The third policy, from San Diego, California, provides in list form what the school system is doing to promote family involvement. It continues in a second section, explaining what the previously mentioned points mean to administrators, staff, and families.

Self-Assessment of Leadership and Commitment

Self-assessment of administrative know-how is an important element in assessing and improving participation by parents. What qualities and skills do you, as a principal, bring to the partnership table? What are your personal strengths and weaknesses?

"The leadership element must be there in order for something to work," says Dietz. "The principal or administrator has [to] be willing and able to build a comfort zone for anyone he or she wants to involve in programs." Fitzmaurice says, "Mobilizing the community begins with committed leaders."

Commitment by staff, parents, and students is also essential. To reinforce responsibilities, school leaders may consider adopting a commitment pledge or contract that specifies each group's responsibilities. A sample of such a contract is Resource 1–5. This student–parent–teacher–administrator agreement asks each party to read and sign, acknowledging that he or she understands what is required to improve student achievement levels. The agreement is an excellent way to define specific responsibilities so that situations do not occur in which one party thinks it is another's job to fulfill specific obligations, as sometimes happens between parents and teachers.

Development of Implementation Plans

For maximum success, programs must be started systematically, with well-defined roles for everyone involved. Comer and Haynes[10] found that each parent-related partnership program is and should be unique. They recommended that the program should encompass a needs assessment, goal statements, prioritization of activities, strategy development, implementation plans, and evaluation tools.[11]

Dietz agrees that administrators must have a multidimensional mental picture of the program before it is initiated. He uses the metaphor of an aircraft to illustrate the point. Administrators, he says, should first envision the program from 10,000 feet, where all elements—people and procedures—are visible. What is the overall flow of resources and information? What resources go into the program, and what is its outcome? Similar assessments should be made at lower levels—at 5,000 feet; 1,000 feet; and ground level. What does each component of the program look like? At ground level, what will be the responsibilities of specific individuals, and how will they be configured?

"This helps assess how well a program is planned and organized," he says.

CONCLUSION

School administrators should not "just start" a family and community involvement program or simply add more programs to their repertoire to say they are addressing the issue. Programs begun in such a haphazard way, at best, will likely yield only average results.

For maximum success, school leaders must put themselves and the involvement programs in question through a rigorous assessment process to determine what the community's needs are, how they can be best addressed, how current programs do and don't meet the needs, and how programs should be structured and evaluated. Understanding the reasons a program works or does not work is the best way to improve it. This approach is also the best way to increase program participation rates and, ultimately, student achievement levels. Schools benefit from written policies to formalize the commitment to involvement. Policies set both standards and expectations that motivate staff members to follow through with program plans.

REFERENCES

1. P.C. Brown, Involving Parents in the Education of Their Children, *Educational Resources Information Center Digest*, ED308988 (Urbana, IL: ERIC Clearinghouse on Elementary and Early Childhood Education, 1989).

2. P. Greenberg, Parents as Partners in Young Children's Development and Education: A New American Fad? Why Does It Matter? *Young Children* 44 (1989): 4, 61–75.

3. K.J. Swick, Parent–Teacher Partnerships, *Educational Resource Information Center Digest*, ED351149 (Urbana, IL: ERIC Clearinghouse on Elementary and Early Childhood Education, 1992).

4. J. Comer and M. Haynes, Parent Involvement in Schools: An Ecological Approach, *Elementary School Journal* 91 (1991): 271–278.

5. J. Epstein, School/Family/Community Partnerships: Caring for the Children We Share, *Phi Delta Kappan* 76 (1995): 701–712.

6. E. Galinsky, Why Are Some Parent–Teacher Relationships Clouded with Difficulties? *Young Children* 45 (1990): 2–3, 38–39.

7. S. Nicolau and C.L. Ramos, *Together Is Better: Building Strong Relationships between Schools and Hispanic Parents* (New York: Hispanic Policy Development Project, 1990).

8. N.F. Chavkin and D.L. Gonzalez, Forging Partnerships between Mexican–American Parents and the Schools, *Educational Resource Information Center Digest*, ED388489 (Charleston, WV: ERIC Clearinghouse on Rural Education and Small Schools, 1995).

9. K. Blanchard and S. Johnson, *One-Minute Manager* (New York: William Morrow & Co., 1992).

10. Comer and Haynes, Parent Involvement in School.

11. Swick, Parent-Teacher Partnerships.

Resource 1–1

Survey on Parent Involvement

Survey of Wisconsin Principals on Parent Involvement at the Middle Level, Part 2

Mark an X after the responses that reflect the current situation at your school and estimate the percentage of families affected.

Percentage of families affected

	Often	Sometimes	Seldom	Never	0–25	26–50	51–75	76–100
1. School provides parents with information on adolescent development.								
2. School provides parents information on parenting middle-level students.								
3. School provides parents with special workshops or meetings on parenting.								
4. School lends parents videotapes or audiotapes of parenting workshops or meetings on parenting.								
5. School provides information on developing positive home conditions that support school learning.								
6. School surveys parents to determine the need for assisting them in parenting middle-level students.								

School–home communications (Mark an X for all responses that apply to your school.)

	Always	Often	Sometimes	Seldom	Never
7. Positive messages about students sent home.					
8. Home notified about student's awards and recognition.					
9. The school contacts the homes of students causing classroom disruptions.					
10. The school contacts the homes of students having academic difficulty.					
11. Teachers have ready access to telephones to communicate with parents during the school day.					

Source: Reprinted with permission from Dietz, M.J. (1992), Principals and Parent Involvement in Wisconsin Middle Level Public Schools. Ph.D. Dissertation, in Madison, WI, University of Wisconsin.

Resource 1–1 continued

12. The school suggests how parents might use home environment (e.g., materials and activities of daily life) to stimulate children's interest in school subjects.								
13. The school's mission is communicated to parents.								
14. The school provides organized opportunities for parents to observe classrooms (not help) for part of a day.								

If the school *does not* have a newsletter, *skip questions 15–23 and go to 24.*

15. Frequency of school newsletter
    A.___Weekly   B.___Monthly   C.___Quarterly   D.__Semester   E.___Other_____

The school newsletter contains (Mark an X for all that apply to your school.)

	Always	Often	Sometimes	Seldom	Never
16. Calendar of school events					
17. Curriculum and program information					
18. Parenting information					
19. School volunteer information					
20. School governance information					
21. Tips to help with homework					
22. Information about issues affecting middle-level students and/or parents					
23. The school mission or philosophy					

24. The *primary* vehicle for sending home messages about your school is
    A.___Student   B.___Mail   C.___Weekly student folder   D.___Other_____

Communications mailed home (Mark an X for all that apply to your school.)

	Always	Often	Sometimes	Seldom	Never	Comments
25. Academic progress/grade reports						
26. Newsletters						
27. Notices of meetings at school						
28. Invitations to student activities						
29. Positive messages about students						
30. Student behavior/performance						
31. PTA/PTO information						
32. Disciplinary information						
33. Surveys						
34. Other:						

35. The percentage of teachers and staff sending/calling home positive messages about students is
   A.___Less than 25%   B.___25–50%   C.___51–75%   D.___More than 75%

Mark an X after all parent involvement practices that apply to *your* school.

36. Academic progress reports are sent home prior to the end of the grading period.	
37. Grade reports include student social and developmental information.	
38. The school has a meeting room/resource room available to parents.	
39. A parent volunteer program for the school is formally organized.	
40. Parents are employed as part of the school's paid noncertified staff (e.g., teacher aides, assistant teachers, parent educators).	
41. The school has a structured format for lending books, workbooks, and other materials to parents to work with their children at home.	
42. The school has a homework telephone hotline.	

Indicate the methods by which your school obtains parent volunteers and the *effectiveness* of each method with an X after the appropriate response.

	Yes	No	Most	Very	Somewhat	Not
43. Principal contacts with parents						
44. Teacher contacts with parents						
45. Newsletter appeals						
46. PTA/PTO committee						
47. Paid school or district coordinator						
48. Other:						

Write the number of volunteers working at your school in the appropriate space after each statement.

	Regular	Occasional	Comments
49. Noninstructional assistance			
50. Tutoring			
51. Assistance in the classroom			
52. Assistance with cocurricular activities			
53. Directing/coaching cocurricular activities			
54. Career education programs			
55. Fund-raising for school programs			
56. Other:			

Resource 1–1 continued

What is the frequency of the following at your school? (Mark an X for all that apply.)

	Quarterly	Semiannually	Annually	Never
57. The school provides staff development for teachers to work with parent volunteers.				
58. The school has a program(s) to recognize parent volunteers.				
59. The school provides parents with information about goals for student academic performance.				
60. The school provides parents with structured ways to comment on school's communications with the home (e.g., mailed/take-home survey, phone survey).				
61. The school gathers information concerning the level and frequency of parent participation in school programs.				
62. The school has formal parent–teacher conference day(s).				

63. The percentage of parents attending parent–teacher conferences is:
    A.___Less than 25%   B.___25–50%   C.___51–75%   D.___More than 75%

What is the frequency of the following at your school? (Mark an X for all that apply.)

	Weekly	Monthly	Quarterly	Semester	Annually	Never
64. The school has a structured program(s) to help parents assist their children with homework.						
65. The school provides parents with information on how to assist their children with learning activities in the home.						
66. The school provides parents with a questionnaire they can use to evaluate their child's progress and provide feedback to the teaching staff.						
67. The teaching staff provides *instruction* for parents to monitor or assist their own children at home on learning activities that are coordinated to the child's class work.						

Parents may receive help and direction from teachers for working at home with students in the following subject areas. (Mark with an X the appropriate response for your school.)

	Always	Often	Sometimes	Seldom	Never	Comments
68. Reading/language arts						
69. Mathematics						
70. Social studies						
71. Science						
72. Other:						

73. The percentage of teaching staff providing help and direction to parents to help students with class work is
   A.___Less than 25%   B.___25–50%   C.___51–75%   D.___More than 75%   E.__Don't know

There are a variety of ways in which parents may participate in the governance of a school. (Mark with an X the frequency of the following statements that apply to your school.)

	Always	Often	Sometimes	Seldom	Never
74. Selecting school staff					
75. Assisting with revising school/district curricula					
76. Planning orientation programs for new students					
77. Developing parenting skills programs					
78. Attending school board meetings					
79. Completing surveys on parent advocacy issues					
80. Other:					

81. The principal arranges for staff and parent groups to meet collectively to discuss school issues.
   A.___Weekly   B.___Monthly   C.__Quarterly   D.__Semester   E.__Never

82. The school has a PTA/PTO.   A.___Yes   B.___No

If NO, skip questions 83–86.

83. The principal meets with PTA/PTO officers.
   A.___Weekly   B.___Monthly   C.___Quarterly   D.___Semester   E.___Never

84. Time of PTA/PTO meetings? A.___Evenings only   B.___Days only   C.___Both days and evenings

85. The percentage of families belonging to the PTA/PTO is
   A.___Less than 25%   B.___25–50%   C.___51–75%   D.___More than 75%

86. Estimate the normal attendance at PTA/PTO meetings.   A. Parents_____   B. Teachers_____

Resource 1–1 continued

Time Management

In this section rate yourself by marking an X in the appropriate space on the time you devote to each area of parent involvement.

	Should spend less time	Spend enough time	Should spend more time
87. Basic obligations of parents—helping families with basic obligations of parenting middle-level students; helping parents to build positive home conditions that support school learning			
88. Basic obligations of the school—promoting school–home communications about school programs and progress			
89. Parent involvement at school—includes volunteer parents who assist teachers, administrators, and children at school both in and out of the classroom			
90. Parent involvement with learning activities at home—helping parents to assist children at home with school work and learning activities coordinated to child's class work			
91. Parent involvement in decision-making roles at the school level (e.g., PTA/PTO, advisory councils, other committees or groups)			

Additional comments on this survey:

_____

_____

_____

_____

_____

Resource 1-2

Learning Together— A Checklist for Schools

Making Your Family–Community Partnership Work

Following are examples of practices and programs that schools and districts can use to encourage family and community support of children's learning. They are meant to be advisory and should be adapted to each school's or district's needs.

Parenting and Family Skills

❑ 1. We sponsor parent education and family learning workshops.

❑ 2. We ask families what types of workshops or informational events they would be interested in attending and what session times are most convenient.

❑ 3. We provide families with information on child development.

❑ 4. We lend families books and tapes on parenting and parent workshops.

❑ 5. We provide families with information about developing home conditions that support school learning.

❑ 6. We survey parents to determine their needs, assign staff members to help address those needs, and work to link parents with community resources.

❑ 7. We have a family resource center or help parents access other resource centers in the community.

❑ 8. We have support groups for families with special interests and needs.

❑ 9. We train staff members and support them in reaching out to all families.

Communicating

❑ 1. We have parent–teacher–student conferences to establish student learning goals for the year.

❑ 2. We listen to parents tell us about their children's strengths and how they learn.

❑ 3. We follow the "Rule of Seven": offering seven different ways that parents and community members can learn about what is happening in the school and comment on it.

❑ 4. Teachers have ready access to telephones to communicate with parents during or after the school day.

❑ 5. Staff members send home positive messages about students.

❑ 6. We make efforts to communicate with fathers.

❑ 7. Parents know the telephone numbers of school staff members and the times teachers are available to take phone calls from parents.

❑ 8. We involve families in student award and recognition events.

❑ 9. We encourage and make provisions for staff members to talk with parents about the child's progress several times each semester.

❑ 10. We communicate the school's mission and expectations for students to parents. The school has a homework hotline or other kind of telephone system.

❑ 11. We provide parents with structured ways to comment on the school's communications, for example, with mailed, phone, or take-home surveys.

Source: Reprinted from *A Checklist for Schools: Making Your Family-Community Partnership Work (Appendix)*, with permission of the Wisconsin Department of Public Instruction, John T. Benson, Superintendent.

Resource 1–2 continued

❏ 12. We have staff members available to assist and support parents in their interactions with the school (i.e., home–school liaisons).

13. We send home communications about
❏ student academic progress
❏ meetings at school
❏ how parents can be involved in student activities
❏ PTA/PTO
❏ student discipline
❏ child development
❏ the curriculum
❏ how parents can be involved as volunteers
❏ how parents can be involved in school governance
❏ how parents can help with homework and encourage learning at home
❏ community resources available to families
❏ how parents can communicate with school staff
❏ the school's philosophy of learning

❏ 14. Staff members make home visits.
❏ 15. *Before* a crisis occurs, we speak directly to parents (does not include leaving messages on answering machines) if students are having academic difficulty or causing classroom disruptions.
❏ 16. We provide copies of school textbooks and publications about the school to the public library.

Learning at Home

❏ 1. We have a structured program to help parents assist their children with homework.
❏ 2. We offer learning activities and events for the whole family.
❏ 3. We invite parents to borrow resources from school libraries for themselves and their families.
❏ 4. We link parents with resources and activities in the community that promote learning.
❏ 5. We give parents questionnaires they can use to evaluate their child's progress and provide feedback to teachers.

❏ 6. School staff and school communications help parents link home learning activities to learning in the classroom.

Volunteering

❏ 1. We encourage families and other community members to attend school events.
❏ 2. We offer youth service learning opportunities for students who want to volunteer in the community.
❏ 3. We help school staff learn how to work with parent and community volunteers.
❏ 4. We *ask* family members how they would like to participate as volunteers at their child's school or in the community.

5. We encourage family and community members to become involved as
❏ participants in site-based management councils
❏ presenters to students on careers and other topics
❏ assistants with art shows, read-aloud events, theater workshops, book swaps, and other activities
❏ tutors/mentors
❏ chaperones on field trips and other class outings
❏ instructional assistants in classrooms, libraries, and computer laboratories
❏ noninstructional assistants
❏ from-the-home contributors of baked goods, assembled materials, typing, etc.

❏ 6. We have a program to recognize school volunteers.
❏ 7. We offer volunteer opportunities for working and single parents.
❏ 8. We gather information about the level and frequency of family and community participation.

Governance and Advocacy

❏ 1. We encourage parents to attend school board meetings.
❏ 2. We assign staff members to help parents address concerns or complaints.
❏ 3. We invite staff and parent groups to meet collaboratively.
❏ 4. We help families advocate for each other.

5. We involve parents in
- ❏ revising school and district curricula
- ❏ planning orientation programs for new families
- ❏ developing parenting skills programs
- ❏ establishing membership for site-based councils
- ❏ hiring staff members

Community Outreach

❏ 1. We act as a source of information and referral about services available in the community for families.

❏ 2. We use a variety of strategies to reach out to adults, families, and children of all ages, races, and socioeconomic backgrounds in the community.

❏ 3. We encourage local civic and service groups to become involved in schools in a variety of ways, such as mentoring students, volunteering, speaking to classes, and helping with fund-raising events.

❏ 4. We encourage staff and students to participate in youth service learning opportunities.

❏ 5. We open our school buildings for use by the community beyond regular school hours.

❏ 6. We work with local chamber of commerce or business partnership council and public library to promote adult literacy.

❏ 7. We have a program with local businesses that enhances student work skills.

❏ 8. We widely publish and disseminate school board meeting notices, summaries, and board policies and agendas and encourage the feedback and participation of community members.

Resource 1–3

Decision-Making Table

1. What learning effects will this proposal have on our children?

	How important is this? (1=low; 5=high)	Yes	No
a. Will they better learn the skills of writing, mathematics, analytical thinking, etc.?			
Which students will learn these skills?			
b. Will they learn more information?			
Which students will?			
What specific information?			
c. Will they learn more useful values and attitudes?			
Which ones will?			
What specific values and attitudes?			
d. What else will they learn?			

2. What other benefits will this proposal have for our children?

	How important is this? (1=low; 5=high)	Yes	No
a. Will they be better prepared for the future?			
To get jobs?			
What kind?			
Who will be better prepared?			
In what way will they be better prepared?			
To *create* jobs? To go to college?			
b. Will the proposal improve their health and safety?			
In what ways?			
How will it do this?			
How will it do this?			
d. Are there other possible benefits?			

Courtesy of the Mountain Institute (formerly Woodlands Mountain Institute). Franklin, West Virginia, phone (304) 358-2401 or www.mountain.org on the World Wide Web.

3. What are the costs of this proposal?

	How important is this? (1 = low; 5 = high)	Yes	No
a. Has anyone prepared a cost estimate for this proposal?			
Has an independent reviewer checked the cost estimates?			
b. What are the indirect costs of this posposed change in terms of demands for support services?			
c. Does this proposal save money in the first three years over the present system?			
How much?			
Does this proposal save money over the long run?			
How much?			
d. Are there other cost considerations?			
Please list.			

4. Will this proposal benefit us and other members of this community?

	How important is this? (1 = low; 5 = high)	Yes	No
a. Will it result in more or better jobs?			
What different jobs will be created?			
How many jobs?			
What is the quality of these jobs?			
Who will get them?			
b. Will members of this community pay lower taxes?			
Which taxes?			
Tax savings per person: $_____ _____%			
c. Will we fell better about ourselves about this community?			
In what way?			
d. As a result of this proposal, will we be better parents?			
In what way?			
e. Are there other benefits for the community?			
What benefits?			

Resource 1–3 continued

5. Will this proposal benefit school administrators, principals, teachers, and other staff?

	How important is this? (1=low; 5=high)	Yes	No
a. Will they be able to do their jobs better?			
Who?			
How?			
b. Will their jobs be easier?			
Whose?			
How?			

6. Will this proposal bring new money into this community?

	How important is this? (1=low; 5=high)	Yes	No
a. In salaries?			
Who will get this money?			
Will stay in the community?			
b. In construction expenditures?			
Who will get this money?			
Will it stay in the community?			
c. For purchases of supplies, equipment, services?			
Who will get this money?			
Will it stay in the community?			

7. Are there ways to change the proposal to improve any of the above factors?

	How important is this? (1=low; 5=high)	Yes	No
a. Changes at the school level?			
b. Changes at the county level?			
c. Waivers that can be requested from the state?			

Resource 1–4

Family–School Partnerships: Make It Board Policy!

Does your school district have a family involvement policy that outlines how parents and family members can expect to be welcomed and involved as partners in the education of their children? Here are three samples that include what commitments the school board will make to enact family partnerships and help parents understand them.

Be sure that parents and other family and community members are included in developing your policy. Or use an action research approach that actively solicits families' opinions, needs, and efforts before and after the policy is written. Their ideas and perspectives will make your policy much more effective and meaningful. Feel free to draw on these sample policies as resources in creating your own district family–school partnership policy.

Sample 1

The following statements regarding family involvement were excerpted from those approved November 23, 1992, by the Milwaukee, Wisconsin, School Board.

1. The _____ School Board acknowledges, affirms, and embraces families as the first and foremost educators of their children.

2. The _____ School Board commits to providing the resources and support needed to increase family knowledge, access, accountability, and decision making.

3. The _____ School Board recognizes that the needs and interests of families must be central to achieving school and district goals.

4. The _____ School Board is committed to respect for and empowerment of all parents and families.

5. The _____ School Board is committed to eliminating barriers to family–school partnerships.

6. The _____ School Board commits to providing the staff and financial resources for a Family Center. The center will serve all parents and families as a point of access for information about parenting skills, learning-at-home techniques, volunteering opportunities, decision-making opportunities, meeting space, and resources available for families in the community.

7. The _____ School Board commits to establishing a Parent–Teacher Association in each school, with the organizational format being determined by parents.

8. The _____ School Board commits to broadening family partnerships in the development of all policies, plans, and procedures that affect the education of children in this district.

9. The _____ School Board acknowledges that parents and families have a right to advocate for their children and be accorded respect by all school district employees.

10. The _____ School Board commits to the creation of written, formalized procedures to resolve parent and family concerns and complaints.

Courtesy of San Diego City Schools, San Diego, California, Tacoma Public Schools, Tacoma, Washington, and Milwaukee Public Schools, Milwaukee, Wisconsin.

Resource 1–4 continued

Sample 2

This policy is adapted from one enacted by the Tacoma, Washington, School District.

School personnel will be at their schools and available to meet with students, parents, and other family members at least 30 minutes before classes start in the morning and at least 30 minutes after school closes in the afternoon, unless a different time has been arranged.

The School Board believes that a child's education is enhanced by a close partnership between the home, the school, and the community. The _____ School District will encourage student achievement by providing a range of opportunities for learning and increasing parenting skills that encourage student achievement.

Parents and families are expected to be involved in their children's education. Each student's family will be expected to dedicate at least 20 hours a year of volunteer time to their children's school(s). In addition, it is the district's goal that parents and families will encourage and participate in their children's academic success. Families should emphasize the importance of students attending school each day, completing homework assignments, valuing education, and following through with suitable learning activities at home.

Families must have a variety of opportunities to work with the schools. The _____ School District will provide these opportunities through many means, including but not limited to personal contacts by staff members, decision making on school committees, volunteering, parent–teacher conferences and open houses, written communications of many kinds, and workshops for families.

A special effort will be made to reach out to families whose primary language is not English, single-parent families, families in cultural transition, and others whose conditions make it difficult to participate in their children's education.

Sample 3

This two-part parent involvement policy statement is used by the San Diego City Schools, California.

The Board of Education recognizes the necessity and value of parent involvement to support student success and academic achievement. In order to ensure collaborative partnerships among schools, parents, and the community, the board working through the administration is committed to

1. involving parents as partners in school governance including shared decision making
2. establishing effective two-way communication with all parents, respecting the diversity and differing needs of families
3. developing strategies and programmatic structures at school to empower parents to participate actively in their children's education
4. providing support and coordination for school staff and parents to implement and sustain meaningful parent involvement from kindergarten through grade 12
5. utilizing schools to connect students and families with community resources that provide educational enrichment and support.

What Does the Policy Mean?

The policy means that
- Parent involvement is recognized as one school improvement strategy that increases student achievement.
- Schools should develop a comprehensive home–school partnership process that provides many ways for parents and school staff to collaborate as
  —communicators of their ideas and concerns
  —supporters of children and the schools
  —learners about school programs, family cultures, and children's progress

—teachers of children and of each other
—advisors, advocates, and decision makers

- School and teacher attitudes and actions affect the level and type of parent involvement.
- The Board of Education and district administration are committed to supporting school site efforts and actions.
- District resources will be organized and distributed in ways that enhance school site programs.
- Training and support must be provided to parents and school staff to help each group acquire the unique and common skills needed to develop a partnership.
- Schools should link school and community resources in ways that will better meet the needs of families.

Resource 1–5

Partners in Learning
Student–Parent–Teacher–Administrator Agreement

(This is a sample. Please feel free to adapt as needed.)

We know that students learn best at _____ School when everyone works together to encourage learning. This agreement is a promise to work together as a team to help _____ achieve in school. Together, we can improve teaching and learning.

As a student, I pledge to

- work as hard as I can on my school assignments
- discuss with my parents what I am learning in school
- respect myself, my family members, and school staff members
- ask my teacher questions when I don't understand something
- use my public or school library frequently
- limit my TV watching and make time for reading

Student signature _____

As a parent, I pledge to

- encourage good study habits, including quiet study time at home
- talk with my child every day about his or her school activities
- reinforce respect for self and others
- be aware of my child's progress in school by attending conferences, reviewing school work, and calling the teacher or school with questions
- volunteer for my child's school or district
- encourage good reading habits by reading to or with my child and by reading myself

- limit my child's TV viewing and help select worthwhile programs

Parent signature _____

As a teacher, I pledge to

- provide motivating and interesting learning experiences in my classroom
- explain my instructional goals and grading system to students and parents
- explain academic and classroom expectations to students and parents
- provide for two-way communication with parents about what children are learning in school and how families can enhance children's learning at home and in the community
- respect the uniqueness of my students and their families
- explore what techniques and materials help each child learn best
- guide students and parents in choosing reading materials and TV programs

Teacher signature _____

As a principal/school administrator, I pledge to

- make sure students and parents feel welcome in school

Courtesy of San Diego City Schools, San Diego, California.

- communicate the school's mission and goals to students and parents
- offer a variety of ways for families to be partners in their children's learning and to support this school
- ensure a safe and nurturing learning environment
- strengthen the partnership among students, parents, and teachers

- act as the instructional leader by supporting teachers in their classrooms
- provide opportunities for learning and development to teachers, families, and community members

Most importantly, we promise to help each other carry out this agreement

Signed on this ____ day of _____, 199__.

CHAPTER 2

Type 1 Involvement: Parenting Skills

To promote type 1 involvement, school leaders should help all families to establish home environments that support children as students.

Parent and family involvement is a key component of education's Goals 2000 program. Goal 8 specifies that by the year 2000, schools "will promote partnerships that will increase parental involvement and participation in promoting the social, emotional and academic growth of children."[1]

A key part of reaching this goal is helping families to meet their basic obligations: to provide a safe, nurturing home environment for children; to support their children's educational endeavors; and to establish appropriate expectations of behavior. Many parents fall short of these goals—some for lack of resources such as time and money, others for lack of knowledge about basic parenting skills. They may be unsure of how to deal with misbehavior, how to set limits, even how to provide for basic nutrition.

Schools can play a significant role in counteracting these problems and helping parents become more effective coaches, disciplinarians, and when appropriate, providers. In turn, children can become more attentive, higher-achieving students because they are better prepared to learn and because they receive consistent messages at home and at school.

How, specifically, can schools address parenting skills? This chapter discusses related issues and strategies.

ISSUES AND STRATEGIES

Changing Family Structure

Despite strong political emphasis on family values, few American families fit the classic mold of *Leave It to Beaver*—a two-parent household led by a bread-winning father and a stay-at-home mother. The US Census Bureau reports that the number of single-parent families grew from 3.8 million in 1970 to 11.4 million in 1994, an increase of 200 percent. Increasingly, students live with relatives who are not their biological parents.

Socioeconomic factors affect students' home life, as well. *Youth Indicators 1993*, a publication by the National Center for Education Statistics, reports that, in 1993, one of five children younger than 18 years old lived in a household in which the income was below the poverty level.[2]

These demographic factors are important, say school leaders, because they influence the amount of time and energy that parents and guardians have to commit to school activities and parenting. As a result, many students lack quality, day-to-day parental supervision and don't arrive at school ready to learn.

Problems Requiring Help with Parenting Skills

Many factors contribute to parents' need for assistance with parenting skills. The following discussion addresses these problems and strategies that can be used in schools to overcome them.

Lack of Time

Parents lack adequate time to refine parenting skills. Most parents, especially single parents, work long hours to support their families. This frequently leaves little time for them to spend with their children and saps their enthusiasm for attending school events and parent workshops.

Gretna R. Willis, coordinator of special instructional programs at the Wicomico County Schools in Salisbury, Maryland, says that conducting parent-related events when and where they are most convenient for parents engages many parents who can't or won't forfeit their personal time to participate in events held at school. "So often we ask them to come to us," she says. "But many of them just don't feel comfortable at school because it dredges up negative memories." Her district's Parents Can Make the Difference program (Resource 2–1) reverses this traditional flow of information by delivering information at the workplace, where parents spend much of their time. The arrangement eliminates many problems that school-based sessions create, including the need for additional child care.

This program is an excellent example of type 1 involvement because it focuses on many parenting skills needed to create a home environment conducive to learning. It is unique because it takes into account parents' time limitations and provides them with information without asking them to make an additional commitment during nonbusiness hours.

Parent sessions can also be organized at community centers and churches, says Principal Jerry Fair, of Milwaukee, Wisconsin. He plans mobile parent–teacher conferences in neighborhoods from which many of his students are bused. More parents participate in teacher conferences when they don't have to travel to the school, he says.

Lack of Parenting Resources

Few parents receive formal training on how to raise a child. Some consult books or magazines for guidance, but for a majority of parents, effective parenting skills are learned by trial and error.

Educators, through training and experience, understand how best to cope with and solve difficult behavioral problems, such as students who defy authority. Consequently, teachers and school staff are in an excellent position to share their collective expertise with parents. Many schools foster this sharing by organizing a variety of parenting publications in parent resource centers. These areas in the school give parents access to books, magazines, journals, and videotapes about both general and specific parenting techniques.

Tom Wailand, a principal in Bradenton, Florida, reserves a portion of the school media center as a parent resource library, where he offers materials on general child development, setting limits, when to be firm and when to give in, and specific education-related topics such as attention deficit disorder. He says many parents, especially first-time parents, often are unsure about how to help their sons and daughters when trouble arises. "I've never talked to a parent who didn't want to help reinforce school discipline at home, but I have talked to many who didn't know how. The resource center is a way to give them the information they need," he says. Assistant Principal Carol Chanter of Casselberry, Florida, says that she tracks use of her parent resource center to determine when it should be open and to learn what specific subjects most interest parents.

Many parent resource centers make materials available for checkout so parents can read at their convenience. But schools are not the only location at which this service can or should be made available. According to Marie Marecek, an elementary guidance counselor and alcohol and drug abuse prevention coordinator in Black River Falls, Wisconsin, parents prefer that checkout materials be available at locations other than the school. "We asked parents where they would be most likely to read and check out materials on parenting, and they chose the public library as opposed to the school," she says.

The El Paso Independent School District in Texas takes a slightly different tack in educating parents. According to materials supplied by Gary Napier, a publication specialist with the district, the Read to Your Babies program aims to promote literacy among preschool-age children and their parents by raising parents' awareness of age-appropriate book titles. Brochures and fliers that identify specific publications are distributed in both English and Spanish and are available by age (e.g., infants to 24 months and toddlers). To complement the publicity campaign, elementary schools hold parent workshops to teach parents techniques for reading to children.

In addition to written materials, many schools offer seminars or minicourses on parenting skills, as well as courses designed to improve parents' personal knowledge and/or job skills. Assistant Principal David Jordan of Henderson, Kentucky, does this through a school-based Parent University program. A variety of sessions are available, including graduation equivalency courses, which are offered in cooperation with the community college. Other examples of minicourses that have been offered through the Parent University: Diffusing Anger; Shared Parenting in Joint Custody; Preparing for College; Everything You've Always Wanted To Know about

Your School Board and School Councils; Creative Thinking Skills; and Parenting Preschoolers with Less Stress and More Success.

The Parent Center at the Murrieta Valley Unified School District in Murrieta, California (Exhibit 2–1), provides a wide range of services to promote type 1 involvement and related information for parents. In addition to regularly scheduled workshops and classes in parenting, the center also offers adult activities such as area trips, resources and referral services, access to technology, and child care while parents use the center. The adult-activity element is a feature not commonly seen in parent programs, but it is an important part of helping parents feel at ease and at peace with themselves, a factor that is reflected in how they deal with their children.

Marecek's Black River Falls School District shares resources with various state and local organizations to offer parent programs through an initiative called Building Collaborative School–Family–Community Involvement (Resource 2–2). The parenting component of the program trains school staff and community members to facilitate small group sessions about parenting skills. Sessions include a review with parents of how they themselves were parented, how that influences relationships with their own children, and how those relationships can be improved. The sessions help parents understand techniques to improve children's self-esteem, which, in turn, improves their attitude and performance at school.

Lack of Basic Needs

For some families, securing basic necessities such as food, shelter, and medical services occupies so much time that parenting becomes a secondary priority. Organizing a system to help families cope with these unfortunate situations puts stu-

Exhibit 2–1   Murrieta Valley, California, Parent Center

The Murrieta Valley Parent Center, California, occupies four rooms at Sivela Middle School, two of which are classrooms. One room is a resource library with books, videotapes, and audiotapes; the other room is a child-care center. The manager of the parent center is Kate Van Horn. The program, which began in 1994, won a 1996 Magna Award for excellence in education.

Parenting classes and resources are the center's main attraction, with 24 courses offered during the 1995–1996 school year and more than 900 titles in the center library, which are available for checkout. The center also offers single evening workshops covering topics that range from home-

work completion strategies to cardiopulmonary resuscitation. For parents looking for peer support, support groups have been organized. Support groups include parents of autistic children and parents of children with attention deficit disorder. Other services available to parents include education in English as a second language; instruction in arts and crafts for family and home projects; access to computers, fax machines, and photocopiers; job preparation workshops; and low-cost child care.

For more information about the parent center, contact manager Kate Van Horn, 24515 Lincoln Avenue, Murrieta, CA 92562; telephone (909) 696-1588.

dents in a better position to learn, and it enables families to devote more attention to education and appropriate parenting techniques, says Principal Fred Ortman. "Children can't learn if they're hungry, tired, or sick."

Many students at Ortman's school in the Los Angeles area come from poverty-stricken or homeless families. Project Healthy Start (Resource 2–3) helps those families meet basic needs by offering nutrition and cooking classes, parenting classes, and laundry and shower facilities. Basic medical services, including immunizations and well-child checkups, are also available. Even though these measures don't address parenting skills per se, they do address basic parenting obligations, which must be met if parents are to have time and opportunity to concentrate on issues such as discipline and academic expectations.

Like Ortman, Principal Elaine Newton of Sierra Vista, Arizona, tends to the needs of severely disadvantaged families through a school wellness center that offers

parenting classes featuring physicians and dentists as presenters. Wellness coordinators also administer a clothing exchange that Newton organized with more affluent surrounding districts. Coordinators solicit and clean donations and leave them in the clothing exchange room for parents to pick up as needed. The center is paid for with federal grant money, a portion of which was also used to hire two Hispanic women to provide assistance to that segment of the school's population.

Commercial Programs and Nonprofit Organizations

State-developed and commercial parent involvement programs, such as Parents as Teachers, are available to school administrators who are willing to invest the necessary time and money. However, commercial programs must be chosen with care, says Mercedes Fitzmaurice, senior research specialist at Research for Better Schools in Philadelphia, Pennsylvania.

She believes that for any program to be successful, administrators must have a specific goal and the program must have been statistically validated. "It's important to narrow the field by thinking of specific criteria [to accomplish] and to practice what's proven," she says.

Regional education research laboratories are excellent sources of information about program statistics. Professional, research, and not-for-profit organizations, such as the Family Involvement Partnership for Learning, are also excellent resources for partnership and collaboration information.[3]

ELEMENTS OF EFFECTIVE PROGRAMS

Labor-intensive, parent-outreach programs can improve both student achievement and, to some degree, a child's general well-being. Powell[4] writes that studies of parent education programs show promising results.

> Evaluations of intensive parent- or family-oriented early-childhood programs serving low-income populations have found positive short-term effects on child competence and maternal behaviors and long-term effects on such family characteristics as level of education, family size, and financial self-support.[5] Others[6] suggest that the magnitude of program effects is associated with the number of program contacts with a family and the range of services offered to the family.[7]

What makes parent education programs effective? Powell[8] cites four essential elements.

1. **Content must be determined by parent needs**. Effective programs use school staff as facilitators who approach parents as equals, rather than as experts. Cochran says that open-ended discussion of parent-initiated topics is preferred to the one-way flow of information provided by traditional lecture sessions, because it ensures that program content does, indeed, meet parents' needs.[9]

2. **Attention to parent and student needs must be balanced**. Although programs may inform parents of ideal ways to address their children's needs, these programs should not focus solely on students. The best outreach programs contain elements that address parents' own social concerns, including interpersonal relationships. Parents who are better able to cope with their own problems can, in turn, give more attention to their children.

3. **Programs must fit the target audience**. Specific programs will not work with all parent groups. Like classroom lesson plans, parent education programs must be tailored to a specific group of parents. Special attention should be given to cultural and socioeconomic characteristics.

4. **Discussion must be parent centered**. Effective adult education takes advantage of participants' experience through discussion of problems and concerns. This process provides parents the opportunity to comprehend information in the context of their own families, as well as to hear new ideas from others in the same situation.[10] The dynamics of the Parents Can Make the Difference program (Resource 2–1) are an excellent example of this strategy.

Relating to Single and Working Parents

In addition to the program elements identified here, Rich[11] recommends that schools use the following guidelines to generate quality relationships with single and working parents.[12]

- Be sensitive to parents' scheduling difficulties, and announce meetings and other events far enough in advance for parents to arrange for leave from work.
- Create a more accepting environment for working and single parents; those undergoing separation, divorce, or remarriage; and those acting as custodial parents.
- Schedule teacher–parent–counselor meetings in the evening, with child care provided.
- Allow open enrollment so children can attend schools near parents' workplaces.
- Provide before- and after-school child care.
- Be careful about canceling school at the last minute due to weather conditions, leaving working parents with no resources for the care of their children.
- Facilitate formation and meeting of peer support groups for teen, single, working, and custodial parents.
- Provide both legal and custodial parents with regular information on their child's classroom activities and any assistance they may need to become involved with the child's learning.

CONCLUSION

Many factors contribute to parents' inability to fully support their children as students. But schools can take steps to help them, through parent education workshops, by collecting and providing resources, and by meeting families halfway—not only by giving parents the information that they ask for, but by taking it to them, rather than expecting them to come to the school.

The experience represented by the resources in this chapter shows that helping parents to become involved in their children's education goes beyond teaching them parenting skills. It also involves helping them to meet basic parenting obligations, such as providing food and shelter. Without these basic necessities, students are ill-prepared to learn. Schools that help families with these problems give them an opportunity to focus time and energy on other issues, such as discipline and expectations. The net result: students are better equipped physically, emotionally, and mentally for the classroom, and their achievement is higher.

REFERENCES

1. *Goals 2000: A Progress Report* (Washington, DC: U.S. Department of Education, May 1995).

2. *Youth Indicators 1993*. Trends in the Well-Being of American Youth. National Center for Education Statistics, Office of Educational Research and Improvement, Washington, DC.

3. V.R. Johnson, *Family Center Guidebook* (Baltimore Center on Families, Communities, Schools, and Children's Learning, Johns Hopkins University, 1996).

4. D.R. Powell, Parent Education and Support Programs, *Educational Resources Information Center Digest*, ED320661 (Urbana, IL: ERIC Clearinghouse on Elementary and Early Childhood Education, 1990).

5. D.R. Powell, *Families and Early Childhood Programs* (Washington, DC: National Association for the Education of Young Children, 1989).

6. C.M. Heinicke et al., Early Intervention in the Family System: A Framework and Review, *Infant Mental Health Journal 9* (1988): 111–141.

7. Powell, Parent Education and Support Programs.

8. Powell, Parent Education and Support Programs.

9. M. Cochran, "Parental Empowerment in Family Matters: Lessons Learned from a Research Program," in *Parent Education as Early Childhood Intervention*, ed. D.R. Powell (Norwood, NJ: Ablex, 1988), 25–50.

10. Powell, Parent Education and Support Programs.

11. D. Rich, *The Forgotten Factor in School Success: The Family. A Policymaker's Guide* (Washington, DC: The Home and School Institute, 1985).

12. C. Ascher, Improving the School–Home Connection for Low-Income Urban Parents, *Educational Resources Information Center Digest*, ED293973 (New York: ERIC Clearinghouse on Urban Education, 1988).

Resource 2–1

Parents Can Make the Difference

Wicomico County Board of Education
Salisbury, Maryland

Issue addressed: Involving parents who can't or won't attend parent-related activities at the school
Agencies involved: School district, local businesses
Type of community: Small city, county-wide population of approximately 75,000
Approximate student enrollment: 13,000
Start date: 1992

School leaders at the Wicomico County Board of Education in Salisbury, Maryland, help parents to strengthen their parenting skills with the Parents Can Make the Difference program, a series of parenting workshops planned by the school district but presented at the sites of local businesses. The program won a 1995 Pinnacle Award for excellence in educational leadership in the community outreach category.

"Parents Can Make the Difference is an attempt to reach parents who may or may not have had success in school and who don't attend events there because they're not comfortable there," says Gretna R. Willis, coordinator of special instructional programs. Instead, the program makes parenting information available to parents where it is most convenient and comfortable for them—at their work sites.

Program Description and Goals

During the program's six weekly seminars, parents learn about building children's self-esteem, promoting positive discipline, helping children be responsible, improving communication, promoting a drug-free life, and fostering success in school. Presenters prepare sessions according to the specified needs of their audience. If a group of parents is concerned with the teenage years, team leaders will focus sessions on that area, says Willis. Another group, however, may discuss the elementary school child.

Basic session structure is planned in advance, but presenters rely heavily on parent discussion of problems, actual situations, and possible solutions. Willis says this flexible, interactive approach has contributed to the program's growth and effectiveness. "One of the reasons this program has been such a success is that we, as school officials, don't go in as 'experts' who have all the answers. We do not say to parents, 'These are the things you should do,'" she says. "Instead, we come in with overall operating principles."

The session focusing on discipline, for example, is built around employees' long-range goals as parents. "We use the comparison that in work we all have goals. And we go to our jobs each day and work toward them," says Willis. "It's the same with parenting. All parents have a long-range picture of what they want their children to be like as adults. What many parents don't realize is that they need to work toward that goal every day."

Materials for the program come from a number of sources, including information provided by

Resource 2–1 continued

other schools and parent-related organizations and materials purchased through the federal Drug-Free Schools Fund. (Because the program includes a drug-prevention element, this funding is permissible.) Other workshop materials are contributed by session presenters who have access to journals and professional materials about parent involvement.

Staff Organization

The workshop presenters—usually school guidance counselors and teachers of special subjects—are divided into two teams of four. Each team is assigned to a business, and each session at a particular work site is led by a different team member.

At the first session, the team leader introduces all session presenters to parents. Each presenter then gives an overview of the session he or she will lead, to help parents understand what's planned. "[This approach] also gives presenters a chance to learn in advance about parents' specific wants, needs, and concerns," says Willis.

Wicomico County uses two teams, both of which present the same topics. With two teams, the school district can serve more businesses. This structure not only minimizes the need for additional staff, but it also allows for last-minute schedule changes. Because two staff people are prepared to present sessions on each topic, a substitute presenter is always available and prepared.

Employer Cooperation

As their contribution to the program, employers provide both a place and time for workshop sessions. Employees typically forgo their regular lunch break to attend the 1-hour sessions. If the break is only 30 or 45 minutes, the company contributes additional time to give employees a full hour for each workshop. And, says Willis, almost all employers provide a meal as an incentive for employees to attend the sessions. Some businesses prefer to hold workshops in the evening for three sessions of 2 hours each.

There is no fee for daytime sessions, because school staff members are being paid by the board of education during the day. Evening sessions, however, cost businesses approximately $600, the cost of reimbursing the school district for stipends paid to school personnel. "This is based on the overall cost of delivering the program," says Willis. "Businesses are told about this up front, and none of them have questioned it."

Sessions are open to all employees, including parents and nonparents. Up to 25 people can attend each session; the average group size is 17.

Garnering support from businesses' top leadership is crucial to the program's success, says Willis. "You simply must have a commitment from the business. Ed Urban, a CEO who served on the committee that developed this program, personally recruited employees at his company to follow through with our pilot project. He also took the first workshop to show his support."

To expand the program, Willis promoted it at meetings of the area's Chamber of Commerce and local business council. Those efforts and word-of-mouth feedback have led to more than 300 parents and 20 area employers participating in the program since it began, she says.

Results

Willis points to ongoing positive feedback as evidence of the program's success. "In addition to a desire for more and longer sessions, two things always appear on workshop evaluation sheets," she says. "One is that parents are grateful that a business cared enough about them to sponsor the program. The second is that the school board cared enough about its parents to come to them and deliver this information."

The program has also affected how businesses perceive specific job skills. "One of the CEOs who attended the communications session said to me, 'It's funny how we pay speakers to come in and train our sales force on how to communicate with customers. I never thought about using those same skills with my own children, but they're just as valid.' Communication principles are communication principles, no matter where they are applied," says Willis.

Sample Materials

Numerous forms and materials are part of the success of the Parents Can Make the Dif-ference program. The following is a sample information flier describing the program. It can be given to interested businesses. For more information about Parents Can Make the Dif-ference, contact the Wicomico County School District at 101 Long Avenue, Salisbury, MD 21802; telephone (410) 548-4727.

Parents Can Make the Difference

WORKSHOP FOR PARENTS IN THE WORKPLACE PROGRAM

Wicomico County Schools
Salisbury, MD 21802-1538

For further information, contact
Mrs. Gretna R. Willis
Board of Education of Wicomico County
P.O. Box 1538
Salisbury, MD 21802-1538
410-548-4727

PARTNERSHIP COMPONENTS

Participating business provides

- a lunch period extended to 1 hour for six sessions for attending employees
- a meeting room
- incentives as company support for em-ployee participation

Wicomico County Board of Education provides

- instructional materials
- staffing to coordinate and conduct the parent workshop

BUSINESS AND PARENT RESPONSE

A first of its kind in Maryland, this program was piloted at Grumman Space and Electronics with the sponsorship of Mr. Ed Urban, director of site operations. The strong, positive response received from parents and the business com-munity indicates the need for and potential of this program for impact on the achievement and citizenship of our children.

> The future of our nation will be decided in our homes. Schools, businesses, and par-ents share a stake in that future and a bond in our children.

Parents Can Make the Difference

Workshop for Parents in the Work-place Program—a business–school partner-ship program of the Wicomico County Board of Education and area businesses, providing parent workshops in
- the workplace
- essential parenting skills
- six 1-hour weekly lunch time sessions
- a parent interaction and discussion-based format
- an inviting, nonjudgmental presentation style by school guidance counselors

that

- brings school personnel to parents in their workplace environment
- builds positive parent–school relation-ships
- meets individual parent-group needs

TOPICS

- Developing responsibility through effec-tive discipline
- Building self-esteem
- Winning cooperation through commu-nication
- Promoting school success
- Helping the child to grow up drug free

Resource 2–1 continued

GOALS

- To impact positively on children and students of our community by assisting parents with effective parenting skills
- To promote greater parent involvement and community support in student achievement and in a drug-free lifestyle

WIN! WIN! WIN!
BENEFITS

For Parent Employees

- Support and assistance in essential parenting skills
- Positive group interaction with coworkers

- Personal growth time free of the constraints of baby-sitting, transportation, and after-work obligations

For Employer

- Beneficial service and support to employees
- Building of workplace morale
- Transfer of positive skills and attitudes to workplace situations

For School

- Increased school involvement and support of business and parents
- Opportunity for reaching parents not already involved in school
- Enhanced relationships of school, business, parents, and students

Resource 2–2

Building Collaborative School–Family–Community Involvement

Black River Falls School District
Black River Falls, Wisconsin

Issue addressed: Building a comprehensive program with a focus on youth development and student assistance programs, parent programs, and community education and curriculum

Agencies involved: School district, parents

Type of community: Rural

Approximate student enrollment: 2,100

Start date: 1990

Program Description and Goals

• *Active Parenting.* In 1990, the Drug-Free Schools Advisory Board in the Black River Falls School District in Wisconsin envisioned building a program that would provide assistance to students, parents, and community education. The result is the current School–Family–Community Involvement Program.

Marie Marecek, elementary counselor and alcohol and other drug abuse coordinator, says the program really took off when the district joined forces with a county-wide partnership of concerned citizens called Together for Jackson County Kids. "We were able to access services, resources, and training to help the vision become a reality with help from this partnership [and from] our relationship with the Western Wisconsin Alcohol and Other Drug Abuse Education Network, the Wisconsin Department of Public Instruction's Count On Me initiative, and a federally funded grant," she says.

According to Marecek, the key to the program is its focus and dedication (1) to helping students become better learners and (2) to encouraging parents to make wise decisions concerning their children. Three main components of the program—parenting sessions, expanding relationships, and student assistance—continue to strengthen the relationship between the school and community.

"Our comprehensive program has evolved to where we are able to use student and parent programs to help not only the kids in school, but members of the community as well," says Marecek.

Program Components

• *Parenting Programs.* One of the exemplary programs at Black River Falls is its Active Parenting program, which started in 1991. "We trained 71 school and community people to facilitate sessions that help parents realize the benefits of complimenting their children and other parenting skills they can use immediately following class," says Marecek. "One woman was so excited about the program, she volunteered to design and produce a brochure we could use to promote the parenting program."

The classes that trained volunteers offer to parents cover topics such as discipline, praise, and communication with children. "One of the exercises parents participate in, for ex-

Resource 2–1 continued

ample, [is to] ask everyone to compliment each person sitting at their table," she explains. "This demonstrates to parents how it feels to receive compliments, as well as the benefits of giving them."

"Another aspect of parenting that's brought out in the sessions is a look back at how the parents were parented," she says. "Then parents are asked to reflect upon how they can use the results of the exercises to improve their relationships with their children."

Part of the Active Parenting program is the development of a resource library of materials on parenting techniques. "We asked parents where they would be most likely to read and check out materials on parenting, and they chose the public library as opposed to the school," she says. "It's encouraging to know that parents participating in the training sessions are also taking advantage of our reading materials."

• *Expanding Relationships Program.* This video/discussion program started in 1992–1993. Community volunteers wrote and developed a videotape exploring the risks children face, behavior problems, and protective measures the school and community can implement. Research was done through a communitywide survey on risk behavior in youths and through personal interviews with people in the community and schools.

"We trained more than 25 volunteers from the community to lead discussions about the videos and topics involved, [such as] underage drinking," says Marecek. "Sessions are planned [for] about four to six times a year and can include up to 12 people."

• *Student Assistance Program.* Marecek says more than 85 community members were educated about the effects of alcohol and drugs on the minds, bodies, families, and classrooms of students. "When students are having trouble learning, chances are there are outside factors affecting their concentration," she says. "By educating people who can help the students through tough situations, we are able to keep more students on line for the education they deserve."

Nearly 40 staff members in the Black River Falls district are qualified to facilitate small groups of students whose social and emotional concerns are interfering with learning. Because the program has been so successful, the district recently received a grant that funded the hiring of a half-time employee to promote, facilitate, and coordinate sessions.

Like most school districts, Marecek says, the Black River Falls district depends on the local weekly newspaper to promote the sessions and programs sponsored through the school. "The paper is good about including a listing about upcoming parenting classes, video discussions, and parenting materials [available] at the library," she says. "We have four lists of the resource materials and ask that every three to four months, one list at a time be promoted. Not only does the newspaper publicize this and feature one book per month, but doctor's offices, the hospital and other human services agencies make the list of publications available to their clients."

Through a grant from the Center for Substance Abuse Prevention, a federal assistance program, the district is able to bring in speakers for presentations on topics that parents, students, and community members want to learn more about. High-profile speaking engagements like these pique curiosity, says Marecek, and bring people out to see what the program is all about.

Planning and Funds

As the program continues to grow, the School–Family–Community Involvement committee searches for other activities to support the school improvement plan, such as parent volunteer programs, a high school newsletter start-up, summer workshops, and family mathematics and reading nights. One of the newest initiatives, however, is the school–family liaison, who was hired by the district under a federal grant.

"A half-time employee has been hired to target a limited number of elementary students and help them build bridges between home and school," she says. "This individual also encourages parents to make maximum use of school and community support systems and resources, [such as] our parenting sessions and library materials. Our hope is that the school district will see how successful the school–family liaison is and see a need to fund such a position for the future."

For more information about the School–Family–Community Involvement Program, contact Black River Falls School District, 301 North 4th Street, Black River Falls, WI 54615; telephone (715) 284-1618.

Resource 2–3

Project Healthy Start

Oleander Elementary School
Fontana, California

Issue addressed: Assisting children and families who are homeless and/or cannot meet the basic life needs of their children, e.g., food, clothing, and shelter
Agencies involved: School district, social service agencies, medical professionals, county and city governments
Type of community: Urban
Approximate student enrollment: 918
Start date: 1993

Program Description

To ease the burden of poverty and homelessness on students, an elementary school in the Los Angeles area annually offers medical and dental care, laundry facilities, nutrition classes, and emergency food to 50–100 families, according to Principal Fred Ortman. The resources are available thanks to Project Healthy Start, a collaborative effort of the city, county, police department, Los Angeles Department of Child and Protective Services, local hospitals, and area drug and alcohol rehabilitation centers.

A blue-ribbon committee of community and school representatives used state grant money to develop the program, which includes a health clinic constructed especially for the program. The clinic at Oleander Elementary School was converted from an unfinished classroom in the school's recent addition and is one of three in the district.

"The facility includes a bathroom facility with a shower, an exam room, a full kitchen with a washer and dryer, and a room equipped for education, training, and [in-house] services [for] parents," says Ortman. "It also includes an office for the child protective services worker, a nurse, and a community aide."

Services

To identify specific services that should be provided by the program, the committee surveyed parents about their needs. "The survey validated our assertion that the basic necessities of life were missing for many children," says Ortman.

Survey findings included the following:
- Forty-three percent of parents lacked adequate access to medical and dental care for their children.
- Only 10 percent of parents said their families received three balanced meals a day.
- Seventy-five percent of parents cited student behavior problems, including the wearing of gang attire and emulation of gang members.
- Eighty-two percent of parents identified the problems of poverty (e.g., lack of utilities, transportation, and sleeping space) as affecting their families.

As a result, the committee planned for three distinct services:
- *A full kitchen and laundry facilities*. Nutrition programs in both English and Spanish are open to parents who don't know how to cook or who know very little about nutrition and meal preparation, says Ortman. "On a regular basis, parents come in and teach other parents how to prepare nutritious meals. This

Resource 2–3 continued

service is provided through a partnership of the county, school, and community." The kitchen is adjacent to a classroom area, making this an easy, convenient activity. Ortman adds that laundry facilities are also available, so students can have their clothes washed.

- *A food distribution program.* For families in need, Project Healthy Start provides food in return for volunteer service. "Participants in the program pay $14 each month and receive $35 worth of groceries in return for two hours of work," says Ortman. Parents are placed according to their interests and abilities, which have included working in a classroom or cleaning the school grounds.
- *A medical examining room.* The school nurse and volunteer physicians perform routine medical services and tests for students in need. Specifically, the school offers well-child checkups, immunizations, and referrals when children need more comprehensive care. Health checkups for students' siblings and dental checkups also are provided.

Center Operation

With the exception of the County Health Department nurse who is a full-time staff member, the clinic is staffed by volunteers from a local health maintenance organization and the medical school at nearby Loma Linda University.

"The head of the nursing service helps us find doctors willing to donate their time to help people in need in the community," says Ortman. "Many of them are private practitioners who want to give something back to the community. We also get people from the county. Some local dentists donate their time as well."

Students are referred by school staff to Project Healthy Start through a case management study team. If a teacher notices that a child is consistently coming to school dirty, for example, that teacher will fill out a criterion paper that identifies for Healthy Start staff what he or she has observed.

Referrals are forwarded to a case study team that determines how to address the student's area of need. The team then routes the referral to the appropriate agency; for example, abuse cases are turned over to child and protective services.

Results

Although conditions for many students and neighborhood residents are better now than in the past, Ortman says there is still "a long way to go." He continues to believe that schools are obligated to help severely disadvantaged students cope with their living situations to improve achievement and learning.

"Just because our students come from the low socioeconomic strata doesn't mean they don't deserve the cleanest and best facilities we can give them," says Ortman. "The child doesn't have control over his or her environment and home life, so our focus was to take care of those children so they can learn. This is a big step in the right direction, for children and families and for us as agencies in the community."

For more information about Project Healthy Start, contact Oleander Elementary School, 8650 Oleander Avenue, Fontana, CA 92335; telephone (909) 357-5700.

CHAPTER 3

Type 2 Involvement: School–Home Communication

To promote type 2 involvement, school leaders should design effective forms of school-to-home and home-to-school communication with all families each year about school programs and their children's progress.

The importance of quality, two-way communication between schools and parents cannot be overstated. Partnerships that lead to higher student achievement are difficult, if not impossible, to establish without it. Given this, it is ironic that so much time is spent teaching students listening and communication skills but that school leaders themselves do a mediocre job of listening and communicating with the community. Some examples are schools with multilingual families that make information available in English only; schools that dismiss or fail to follow up on parent and resident suggestions; schools that hesitate to cooperate with the media; schools that deliver predominantly "bad" news about students rather than "good" news; and schools that don't emphasize teacher communication with parents.

A study of Iowa school districts by Stephen Kleinsmith, assistant superintendent at the Millard Public Schools in Millard, Nebraska, shows that effective communication skills are the most important quality a school administrator can possess (Exhibit 3–1). The study asked school board presidents and superintendents to prioritize a list of 10 leadership qualities. The qualities ranked were stated as follows: values-driven work ethic, champion team builder, communicator, enthusiastic optimist, high expectations of self and others, lifelong learner, one who overcomes adversity, progressive change agent, visionary goal achiever, and willingness to take risks. Both superintendents and board presidents ranked communication as the most important trait a school leader could have.

"I consider this [these results] a clear reflection of the demands on school leaders and the need for them to work with the community around them," Kleinsmith says.

This chapter, which focuses on methods that school administrators can use to improve relations with the community, addresses school-to-community communication and home-to-school communication. Among the topics discussed are

- crafting school newsletters
- preparing for parent–teacher conferences
- increasing communication through technology
- improving media relations
- inviting parent–community communication
- implementing an open-door policy

SCHOOL-TO-COMMUNITY COMMUNICATION

Although the bulk of a school's outgoing communication informs parents of activity schedules, policy changes, and important dates, school leaders also must

Exhibit 3–1 Leadership Characteristics

Analysis of the study data suggests that Iowa public school board presidents and school superintendents have highly similar views regarding the leadership characteristics needed for success in the superintendency. Furthermore, the following data indicate that school district enrollment size has little bearing on the ranking of those characteristics. Assuming that the differences in the ranking of each quality among the school districts could be as great as 9, these similarities are significant. Analysis showed a statistically strong correlation between the ranks perceived by school board presidents and superintendents, regardless of the size of the school district.

Rank Order of Leadership Characteristics by Small School District Board Presidents and Superintendents

Leadership Characteristics	Board President (rank)	Superintendent (rank)
Values-Driven Work Ethic	5	2
Champion Team Builder	2	4
Communicator	1	1
Enthusiastic Optimist	6	8
High Expectations of Self and Others	3	3
Lifelong Learner	8	10
One Who Overcomes Adversity	9	9
Progressive Change Agent	7	7
Visionary Goal Achiever	4	5
Willingness To Take Risk	10	6

Rank Order of Leadership Characteristics by Medium School District Board Presidents and Superintendents

Leadership Characteristics	Board President (rank)	Superintendent (rank)
Values-Driven Work Ethic	3	5
Champion Team Builder	4.5	3
Communicator	4.5	1
Enthusiastic Optimist	7	7
High Expectations of Self and Others	1	2
Lifelong Learner	8	9
One Who Overcomes Adversity	10	10
Progressive Change Agent	6	6
Visionary Goal Achiever	2	4
Willingness To Take Risk	9	8

Rank Order of Leadership Characteristics by Large School District Board Presidents and Superintendents

Leadership Characteristics	Board President (rank)	Superintendent (rank)
Values-Driven Work Ethic	4.5	4
Champion Team Builder	1	3
Communicator	2	2
Enthusiastic Optimist	9	9
High Expectations of Self and Others	3	6
Lifelong Learner	6	7
One Who Overcomes Adversity	10	10
Progressive Change Agent	8	5
Visionary Goal Achiever	4.5	1
Willingness To Take Risk	7	8

Courtesy of Millard Public Schools, Omaha, Nebraska.

refine skills for dealing with other external audiences, including the business community, government and social service agencies, media representatives, and community residents.

The key to quality communication with these audiences is to vary the method of delivery. All methods available should be used to convey information and prepare the message in multiple languages. These methods include print and video, audio, and electronic techniques. The following is a discussion of various ways in which schools tell their stories to parents and the community.

Crafting Quality Newsletters

Newsletters are the most common way schools communicate with external audiences. Principal Michael Dietz reports that they also are considered the most reliable source of information, according to a telephone survey of parents at Lake Shore Middle School in Mequon, Wisconsin. Every fourth individual listed in the parent registry was asked what he or she liked best about school communications. The school's monthly newsletter scored consistently well.

What makes a first-class newsletter? Good information, yes. But Superintendent Jon Rednak says appearance is as important as content. "If teachers and educators want to be looked upon in a more professional manner, they need to provide top-quality, professional looking information to parents and community residents."

Dietz, however, says newsletters don't have to be flashy and polished to get the job done. "They simply need to have the information in them that parents want."

The best newsletters strike a balance between these two positions. They also follow general publication rules.

Know the audience. All communication must be tailored to the audience and its information needs. Technical jargon, which often peppers internal communications to faculty and staff, means little to parents and community members.

However, it is equally important not to oversimplify communications. "Talking down to people puts them off as much as talking above them," says Kleinsmith. Both he and Rednak say optimum readability is best achieved by asking members of the target audience to review a draft copy of communications.

"If a written report isn't communicating what you actually mean, it must be changed," says Rednak, "or people will be left to make assumptions about what it means. And assumptions often turn into rumors, which can have a tremendously negative effect on the district's relationship with the community." He describes a past district report outlining an elementary school reorganization as "so unclear, [that] people completely misunderstood what we were thinking of doing." The board reacted by dismissing the entire idea.

Review of draft copy is especially valuable when communication is related to a controversial issue. Kleinsmith says, "Readers can provide extremely valuable insight as to whether the content of the communication will be inflammatory. Once you go public with something, you can't go back—so you need a variety of people to look at communications prior to their final draft."

To assess readers' specific communication wants and needs, Kleinsmith conducts focus groups. He randomly invites members of a given publication's target audience to participate, then sends them copies of the publication and preparation instructions in advance of the meeting. During the session, he compares information currently provided in the publication with information that participants described as most important.

In combination with focus groups, Kleinsmith invites wide-scale reader feedback on school publications by placing in all communications a standing invitation for readers to communicate their opinions. A variety of response methods, including telephone, fax, mail, or electronic mail (e-mail), are encouraged.

Publish in more than one language. Part of meeting audience needs is making communications available to everyone in the audience, not just those who speak English. Principal Fred Ortman says his school in the Los Angeles area produces all communications, whether sent to parents or the media, in both English and Spanish.

"Our school is 70 percent Hispanic, and we need to be welcoming to all parents, many of whom speak only Spanish," he says. "By making our communication user friendly, we're doing our best not to exclude families from our school."

Principal Brenda Dykes provides Spanish translators at meetings of the Parent–Teacher Organization. Because of this practice, she says more than 200 parents often attend the meetings.

Include only essential information. Long work hours for parents and busy extracurricular schedules for students mean that "the shorter and sweeter a story is, the better it is," says Kleinsmith. "People will read something that makes its point quickly and clearly, but they probably won't read a lengthy piece unless it's about a really hot topic."

To hold readers' attention, he recommends using bullet-style lists and short summaries of what administrative decisions mean to parents, instead of in-depth descriptions of problems and issues. Repeated features, such as lunch menus and calendars of events, should always be placed in the same place in the publication. Readers who always look for specific information become accustomed to looking in the same location for it. Moving those features is

both frustrating and inconvenient to the reader.

Balance attention to people and policy. Many school newsletters tend to be very procedure oriented, as opposed to stressing student and teacher achievement, says Amy Friedman, communications coordinator at Millard Public Schools in Millard, Nebraska. "This is not to say that newsletters shouldn't be used as vehicles to pass along procedural information. But people like to read about people."

Use an easy-to-read format. Large quantities of information are not necessarily what the audience wants, says Friedman, especially if it is difficult to read. "There's a misconception that a lot of communication is the best communication, so [schools] develop 10- to 12-page newsletters full of blocks of copy."

The problem, however, is that to readers with low reading skills and readers who did not enjoy school, this format may appear intimidating and difficult. Consequently, these individuals may only skim the information or, more likely, she says, not even look at it. "Our [district] goal is to use more graphics in our publications and to present information in a two-column format. We're also trying to use more white space," says Friedman.

Plan ahead. Appeal is broadened by mapping out which topics will be part of each newsletter (e.g., even balance of emphasis on academics and athletics). This approach also gives the administrator additional control over each issue's content, especially when writing and/or production is turned over to staff or parent volunteers. "When I require staff to write stories about their areas of responsibility, I tell them which month I plan for the article to appear and give them a specific date that I want the completed story turned in," says Kleinsmith.

Proofread. Although it may seem like a small, commonsense detail, proofreading is easily sacrificed to meet deadlines. But few things can make a school look as unprofessional as misspellings and incorrect sentence structure. (Those are, after all, things schools are supposed to be teaching.)

Include the school logo. This technique is a lesson that schools can learn from businesses, says Friedman. "[Businesses] make sure their logos appear on everything associated with them. The audience learns to recognize the logo and, as that happens, the organization's identity strengthens."

Providing Urgent Information through News Releases

When information must be communicated quickly, Kleinsmith recommends using news releases to parents. These one-page documents are different from news releases sent to the media and from other communications between school and home, which lends urgency and importance.

However, parent news releases must be used sparingly and must contain timely and important information. Anything related to student safety and security, for example, is fair game for a parent news release. "If there's a change in how students will be dismissed during bouts of inclement weather and it's the middle of winter, we put that in a news release, because it may apply the very next day," says Kleinsmith.

Establishing Individual Contact

In addition to the general dissemination of information via newsletters, individual communication with parents is also necessary. A specially designed parent communication room reminds teachers of this responsibility and provides them with resources to follow through with it, says Assistant Principal Kevin Davis, of Carmel, Indiana. The room includes several telephones, samples of both positive and negative letters that teachers may use as models, envelopes, mailing addresses, and telephone records.

"We're telling our teachers, 'If you have a problem with a student, don't dawdle. Let parents know about it. If you have something positive to share, don't put that off either. Come here and make contact,'" he says.

At a Tom Bean, Texas, elementary school, each teacher has a telephone and a list of parents' telephone numbers in the classroom. "Not only do the phones help teachers solve discipline problems and communicate positive news, they also cut down on paperwork and phone duties for the office staff," says Principal Patty Madison.

Supplying Information through Effective Handbooks

Handbooks are one of the most efficient ways for schools to communicate information about programs, facilities, policies, and procedures. Generally, two styles of handbooks exist: the school–parent handbook distributed by individual schools and a district handbook available through the central district office.

A strong parent focus makes parent handbooks most appealing, says Assistant Principal David Jordan, of Henderson, Kentucky. His school's handbook begins with a letter inviting parents to participate in school activities, followed by pages about education and family-related topics, including helping children succeed in school, helping children adjust to a parent's remarriage, learning to talk with children, and guidelines for setting rules. "Parents read this section more closely than they do the information geared to students [that appears later in the handbook]," he says.

Principal Nancy Renfro, of Indian Head, Maryland, summarizes important policy-related information on two pages in her handbook that she calls the Quick Reference Section. Parents enjoy the convenience of having policy details in one place, she says, rather than having to use an index to locate specific information.

Other handbook practices that can set the tone of the parent–school relationship include:

- a passage in the welcome letter emphasizing parents' roles and responsibilities in children's success or failure in school
- information on school contacts that is prominently displayed (front cover, back cover, boldface type)
- an open letter from faculty inviting parent dialogue
- information on contacting staff members, organized by department and grade level, including guidance counselors
- dates of parent–teacher conferences, a summary of their importance, and expectations for them
- an introduction to the volunteer program and volunteer opportunities
- a building map to guide visitors
- a calendar of school activities
- handbooks available in languages other than English

Like parent handbooks, district handbooks are an excellent means of communicating with the community at large, as well as families that are new to the district and trying to choose a school. And, like parent handbooks, these publications can be put together in a variety of ways.

The Fort Wayne, Indiana, school district publishes a handbook annually as a guide to its School Choice Fair (Resource 3–1), a 1-day event open to the public, in which all of the district's schools promote curriculum and activities to parents and community members. The 28-page booklet for the 1995 fair begins with information about each school in the district, including the school address and telephone number, the name of the principal, and unique features of the school listed in bullet form. In the outside margin area of each page are snippets of information, such as the process for applying to a school. Also included in the book is a matrix providing an at-a-glance summary of the location and features of each school, a district map, enrollment forms for both elementary and secondary schools, and short synopses of other district programs, including adult and continuing education, career education, alternative learning, special education, and community programs.

The fair is an outstanding way for schools to promote type 2 involvement by telling their stories through a variety of media. Conversely, it is an excellent means for parents and residents to ask questions and communicate with the schools. The event also addresses growing concern among public schools about competition from private schools, because it is an opportunity to advertise the strengths of the public schools.

All handbooks should be updated annually. To help identify specific items that need clarification or that were previously omitted, Principal Patricia Andrews, of Wausau, Wisconsin, each year asks parents who are new to the school to keep a running list of school-related problems, questions, and subjects they wish they had known about. She uses this information as a guide to rewrite the handbook.

At a Rochester, New York, elementary school, parents receive a new handbook each year. Principal Marie Ginther inserts a letter in the handbooks that asks parents how the publication can be improved.

"They often tell us they feel something has been overlooked or ask us to clarify some policy for them. This feedback has made our handbook more understandable," she says.

Preparing for Parent–Teacher Conferences

Even though most schools require parents to attend parent–teacher conferences at least once a year, these conferences remain an underused method of school-to-home communication.

Among the factors that contribute to this situation is the lack of preparation for the event. Most conferences are well organized, and teachers are well prepared. Frequently, however, little is done to shrink the communication gap between parents and staff. Most parents, for instance, view teachers as "experts" and hesitate to ask questions of them. Other parents don't understand what questions they should be asking. On the other hand, teachers often speak over parents' heads and fail to solicit their opinions and cooperation on improving student achievement.

These problems can be alleviated when administrators help both teachers and parents to prepare for conference meetings. Education Consultants Joan S. Wolf, of the University of Utah, and Tom Stephens, executive director at the School Study Council of Ohio, say that for conference communication, teachers should be prepared in four areas.

1. *Building rapport with parents*. Teachers must remember first and foremost that they and parents share the same goal: a well-educated, well-adjusted child. They also must be sensitive to the fact that parents view children as an extension of themselves. Therefore, teachers should exercise caution when discussing students' strengths and weaknesses. Wolf and Stephens also recommend using small talk to break the ice at conference sessions and stress that, to avoid resurrecting uncomfortable memories of school, teachers should not ask parents to sit in small child-size furniture.

2. *Obtaining information from parents*. Unlike teachers, who tend to talk too much during conferences, parents vary in their willingness to speak, say Wolf and Stephens. Teachers are best served by asking open-ended questions that cannot be answered with a "yes" or "no." For example, ask, "Which activities has Felix mentioned lately?" Teachers should then focus on listening, and guard against interrupting the parent or talking over the ends of the parent's sentences.

3. *Providing parents with information*. Teachers should offer information about a student's progress on the basis of the parent's reaction, say Wolf and Stephens. If conversation is difficult and nonproductive, teachers have three options.

   a. Close the conference and reschedule it for another time.

   b. Complete the conference, covering all areas planned, expecting little if any change as a result.

   c. Repeat the first two steps—building rapport and obtaining information—hoping that rapport will improve.

When the conference flows smoothly, teachers can proceed with a review of the student's progress. For specific tips on how best to present this information, see Exhibit 3–2, which is a simple checklist reminding teachers how to best interact with parents. The list can be used as a guide to preparation of materials for a conference and can be reviewed quickly before the actual meeting.

Exhibit 3–2   Parent–Teacher Conference Dos and Don'ts

When giving parents information about student's progress, follow these rules for best results.

DO

- Organize information into broad categories. Have an agenda, and when appropriate, provide an outline for parents to follow.
- Begin with positive information.
- Cite specific examples related to the shared information.
- Encourage parents to discuss each point, and clarify it as needed.
- Have examples of the student's work, dated and noting progress.
- Emphasize how instruction is individualized.
- Encourage parents to ask questions.
- Listen to what parents have to say. Try to understand them before making yourself understood.

DON'T

- Overwhelm parents with information.
- Use educational jargon.
- Speculate on why there are difficulties.
- Be evasive. If you don't know the answer, admit it.
- Defend an archaic grading system.
- Predict life's successes from any test scores or other data.
- Describe problems to parents. They are not interested in why teachers are unable to help the student.

4. *Summarizing and follow-up.* Many teachers mistakenly end the conference without summarizing how the parent and teacher will cooperate to improve student achievement and/or behavior. Wolf and Stephens say that teachers should alert parents to time constraints when the conference begins.

Teachers should also be reminded that for successful conferences, parents also need guidance on how to prepare for them, for example, what to ask and what to listen for. Some teachers send parents lists of questions they can ask during the conference or questions they can ask of their children before the conference. Samples developed by the Wisconsin Department of Instruction are shown in Resources 3–2 and 3–3. Resource 3–2 is a letter from the teacher to the parent explaining how the parent can prepare for the conference, as

well as some questions that a teacher may ask. This strategy maximizes use of limited conference time, because parents can arrive with information that teachers need, rather than having to give whatever answer comes to them. Resource 3–3 is a list of suggested questions that parents can ask of teachers, which teachers can send home prior to a conference.

To help parents think specifically about the student's interests and how they may apply to school, Assistant Superintendent Kleinsmith suggests that parents write notes about the student's hobbies and activities. Parents should also note school rules or policies affecting the student and ask if there is anything the student would like the parent to ask during the conference.

Improving Conference Attendance by Parents

Conference preparation means nothing if parents do not participate in the conferences. Many principals say that offering conference times other than during the school day improves the attendance rate, as does school-provided transportation to and from the conference site. Principal Jerry Fair says that about 65 percent of students at his Milwaukee, Wisconsin, school are bused from as far away as 13 miles, adding to the indifference many parents feel about attending conferences. "Many just won't make the trip," he says.

Fair now holds conferences for 1 day at the school, where parents in the school's immediate neighborhood can attend, and on the following day moves the conference location to a church in the neighborhood from which students are bused. The result has been a dramatic increase in attendance.

For other parents, the issue preventing them from attending conferences is not disinterest, but homemaking and childcare obligations. The Parent–Teacher Association at Assistant Principal Carol Chanter's school addresses these obligations by providing a low-cost meal and free baby-sitting service to parents who attend the evening sessions. Parents can eat in the cafeteria with their children before meeting with teachers, and the free baby sitters make it possible for more parents to attend.

Increasing Communication through Technology

Increased computer resources, including access to Internet and World Wide Web and modernized telephone systems, are expanding the communication of schools with both internal and external audiences. For example, e-mail allows school administrators to send and receive information 24-hours a day. The World Wide Web allows schools to post and update information that can be accessed from any computer with an Internet navigation program. Remote-access video can link students in different locations for a single classroom presentation and discussion.

These and other technologies should be as much a part of a school's communication repertoire as newsletters, newspapers, radio, and television, says Communications Coordinator Friedman. As people become more sophisticated with home computers and other new technology, they will look to these sources of information as much as they have relied on traditional communication methods in the past. Friedman's district already uses e-mail to keep staff apprised of school news and to dispel rumors. When rumors about use of a specific drug began swirling, Friedman issued an electronic memo to principals, providing information about the drug and advising them on how to respond to questions about it. "I heard from several of them that the immediate communication helped them to respond to parents and to reassure them that no problems existed," she says.

For obvious reasons, e-mail works best with small, well-defined audiences, such as staff members, board members, Parent–Teacher Organizations, and individual clubs. To reach more global audiences, such as parents or the community at large, it is more effective to use a home page on the World Wide Web.

Friedman says the Millard, Nebraska, school district is developing a web site that provides Internet surfers with information about district activities and also allows readers to give feedback, ask questions, and share opinions about school issues and activities. "We want to give readers the option of clicking on a feedback category that allows them to communicate with individual schools or the central district office," she says.

For high useability of a web site, only a few photos should be used, and the page should be kept current. The time needed to download multiple photographs will frustrate users who want to get in and out of the web site quickly.

To browse school home pages, consult the School Home Page Registry on the World Wide Web. Most schools with home pages are accessible alphabetically by state. The address is <http://web66.coled.umn. edu/schools.html>. For a list of potential items for a web site, see Exhibit 3–3, which enumerates more than 20 ideas that other school home pages have included.

Internet access also makes schools excellent community resources for computer information and training and is an effective vehicle for bringing nonparent residents into the school. The Beachwood Public School District in suburban Cleveland, Ohio, is promoting communitywide computer literacy through beginning and intermediate computer courses for senior citizens as part of its Elderclass program

(Resource 3–4). The program, which offers services in addition to the computer courses, has wide appeal to older adult community members and generates a large amount of school support from that group.

Superintendent Rednak's Pennsylvania district opens its high school library as part of the Second Shift program that makes school facilities available to the public after normal business hours. The library is one of the few places where any member of the public can use a computer and access Internet resources. Volunteers from the school's coaching staff, Parent–Teacher Association, booster clubs, and faculty supervise the library during late-afternoon and evening hours, when students, parents, and community residents can take advantage of the technology available.

Video technology should also be considered a valuable communication tool, says Andrew Thomas, community rela-

---

Exhibit 3–3   Web Site Ideas

Consider the following elements when developing your school's home page on the World Wide Web:

- School activity calendar
- Staff directory with individual telephone numbers and e-mail addresses
- Main telephone number and street address of school
- List and contact information for school administrators and department heads
- Student–parent handbook
- Recent editions of school publications (e.g., school newsletter, school newspaper, school-oriented news stories)
- Lunch menus
- Event and activity notices
- School calendar
- Building map and virtual tour
- Volunteer opportunities
- Samples of student work from unique programs or award-winning projects
- Parenting tips and strategies

- Mission statement
- Scholarship opportunities
- E-mail communication opportunities
- District information
- Links to other education-related sites
- School history
- Student government news
- Children's activities
- Alumni news and updates
- Department news (e.g., athletics, academics, drama, and band)
- Club information
- PTA/PTO information
- Awards and scholarship updates
- School neighborhood and city information
- Principal's message
- Homework and discipline policies

tions coordinator at the Canandaigua City Schools in Canandaigua, New York. His district created a videotape for elementary school orientation that gives newcomers a first-person look at the building's layout, a summary of rules and procedures, and a glimpse of the school's atmosphere.

"We felt that with VCRs in every home and more people turning to video as a way of gaining knowledge, many parents would have a real use for a product like this," he says. "In the past, when someone inquired about the school, we sent him or her a map and some literature. That's valuable. But with video you have a medium that shows pictures of what the school actually looks like and how daily events happen. We believe that if parents and students can watch together in the comfort of their own living rooms, students will feel a lot better about coming to school on their first day."

Resource 3–5 is a full outline of Thomas' Discover the Excellence program, which won a 1995 Pinnacle Award for excellence in education and community outreach. It describes in detail how the videotape is used and its benefits.

Improving Media Relations

Of all external audiences, the media are perhaps the most threatening to school administrators. But that fear is overblown, says Friedman. "The media [are] very accessible and willing to cover both the good news and the bad news. It's a misperception that [they are] only interested in schools when there's an incident of violence," she says.

Ongoing communication with reporters can help administrators ensure that their schools receive fair, even news coverage. An easy way to begin building, or refining, a cooperative relationship is to keep the media updated on school activi-

ties through news releases. For optimum results, these documents should have the following qualities.

1. *Succinctness.* The time and space allotted to school news likely will be limited, Kleinsmith says. Economy of language is essential. To provide detailed information without short-changing the opportunity for coverage, Kleinsmith recommends writing news releases in two parts. On the first page, write the bare bones summary. Then attach a more lengthy, detailed message. "If [reporters] have time or space, they can elaborate," he says.

2. *Newsworthy content.* Friedman says principals should apply the "what, so what rule" before releasing information to the media. She advises teachers and administrators to ask themselves, "What is going on?" and follow that question with "So what? What makes this different or important, and why should others be interested?"

   "If [teachers and administrators] come up with a good answer to both questions, then the event is probably newsworthy, and a release should be drafted," she says. "Items also have to be things that aren't standard school activities. Writing that parent–teacher conferences are coming up, for example, is not something the media [are] interested in."

3. *Adequate contact information.* News releases should feature at least two people whom reporters can contact for further information, says Kleinsmith. "If a reporter can't reach the first contact, your school won't automatically lose the opportunity for exposure. The reporter already has the name and number of a second contact person."

4. *Suited to the medium.* Administrators with media savvy tailor messages to the appropriate medium, says Friedman. "Television likes things with visual appeal. Some events [that] don't seem groundbreaking are things that television really jumps on because they can get vivid, interesting pictures," she says.

Friedman cites local television stations' "huge" response to beach party lunches held at several district locations, where students bring beach towels to sit on in the gymnasium or cafeteria during the lunch period. "[Television stations] liked the visual appeal of this event in contrast with the winter weather outside," she says.

School officials must realize that news coverage won't always be rosy, says Rednak, but openness and a cooperative attitude yield dividends in the long run. He says the local media's attitude toward his school district changed almost immediately after he discontinued his predecessor's practice of never giving out copies of the school district's proposed budget. "Reporters had a lot of questions the first year [I gave them this information]. But the second year they just accepted the information and wrote a very positive story about the district."

Communicating in Crisis Situations

Facing the media during a crisis is always awkward for school leaders, says Friedman, but not answering reporters' questions likely will worsen an already bad situation.

"I can't stress enough that people not wait for reporters to go away, because they won't. The media [are] very persistent, and if you won't talk, they will find someone who will talk. And it may not be from your point of view. It's very impor-

tant to speak soon so you don't lose the public's trust," she says.

Information should be presented calmly, systematically, and as it becomes available. Generally, Friedman says administrators should give the facts of what happened and what actions were taken and conclude with the steps the school is taking to prevent the situation from recurring. "It's important that you be seen as someone who is taking charge and accepting responsibility. This is how you maintain people's trust," she says.

As soon as school officials learn of a problem, they should begin gathering facts and informing the media of when they plan to make a formal statement about the situation. Scheduling a press conference buys time to find out what happened and minimizes media-related distractions during the fact-gathering process. "Reporters will understand if you say you will get back to them when you know more and then follow through," says Friedman.

Delaying a meeting with the media or refusing to comment, however, are serious mistakes that fuel the public rumor mill. In crisis situations, says Friedman, some comment is almost always better than none. "Whatever you do, never say, 'No comment.' What this means in the public's eye is that you're hiding something."

Despite the inherent negativity, a crisis is actually an opportunity for a school and its leaders to shine in the public eye, says Friedman. "Everyone is watching. A school district can use that time to demonstrate its organization, professionalism, and resiliency." She adds that ongoing media communication is also essential to the healing process a school must experience after a crisis.

"It's important to continue to sell yourself and talk about what's good in the schools. This helps the public reconnect with what they knew was good about the schools before anything happened," she says. Periodically informing the media of progress on long-range plans to solve the crisis-provoking situation is also strong follow-up strategy. When possible, the media should be encouraged to produce a follow-up story about how the school or district has been improved since the original incident.

HOME-TO-SCHOOL COMMUNICATION

Many school leaders are effective at keeping parents and the community informed about activities, programs, and achievements. Unfortunately, a significant number do a poor job of inviting parent input and listening to parent comments.

Methods of Communication

The responsibility for creating and maintaining two-way communication belongs very much to schools. Rarely will parents or community members initiate communication without first being invited to do so or without having received some indication that someone is listening to them. School leaders convey this message in different ways.

Open forums. Randy Pratt, principal in Butler, New Jersey, invites the community to participate in regular "forums" at his building, where residents can ask about school programs and air concerns about expenses and other school issues. As a result of this communication, Pratt says, the school has the neighborhood's confidence and "parents are more supportive and involved and feel they're listened to."

School administrators in Fort Plain, New York, use neighborhood meetings (Resource 3–6) to invite parent and community feedback about school district news and issues, which takes place in the homes of parents and residents. The strategy, says Superintendent and Principal John Metallo, reaches some individuals who would not feel comfortable visiting the school or asking questions there. "Since the meeting is on 'private turf,' people are less intimidated by school staff and more at ease with themselves."

Clip-out telephone information. The annual report published by the Columbia Borough School District in Pennsylvania includes a coupon identifying key personnel and their telephone numbers. The coupon can be quickly clipped and posted for easy reference should someone have a question or concern, says Superintendent Rednak.

Published invitations. School leaders who have newsletter columns should use them as vehicles to invite communication, says Kleinsmith. "It's important to remind readers that the school district has an open-door policy and that its staff members are there to serve the public. Administrators should encourage parents to visit personally if they have specific questions or problems they would like addressed."

Community presence. Visibility at community events and membership in organizations make school officials more approachable. "It communicates that you care about the community and want to be part of it. You're not just sitting at your desk collecting a paycheck," says Rednak.

Business reply cards. As part of the published district calendar, the Millard Public Schools include two business reply inserts on which individuals can indicate their interest in school activities or submit general comments. When received at the school, the cards are forwarded to the appropriate staff person, who contacts the sender for more detailed information, says Kleinsmith.

Key communicators group. This popular community relations technique, in which schools recruit residents to act as purveyors of school-related information, keeps many administrators abreast of what is said in the community about their schools.

For maximum benefit, enemies should be invited to participate in these groups, says Rednak. Individuals who question school actions bring a devil's advocate perspective to discussions and may bring issues to light that previously may not have been closely examined. "The outcome is that those particular people feel they are part of the school system because they're participating. And we make better decisions because all angles of an issue are explored," he says.

Rednak also advocates limiting the length of time an individual can serve as a key communicator for a school. In his district, the maximum term is 2 years. This policy helps to avoid the possibility of the key communicator group being perceived as his "personal 'yes' group," he says.

Community surveys. When it is necessary to gather information on a larger scale, telephone or direct mail surveys are effective ways to collect opinions about a school.

Written surveys should be simple, says Friedman, and short—no more than one page. Multiple-choice questions are preferable to other types, but they should be somewhat open ended. If respondents disagree with all possible choices, there should be space to write in a more accurate response.

A structured telephone interview, in which callers ask individuals predetermined questions, can reveal how a school's communication efforts are received, as well as which communication methods are most effective.

Parent feedback gained through a telephone survey changed the Millard Public Schools' calendar, says Friedman. "The board [set the date for the start of school] believing that it was important to parents to have the semester end before the holidays. We called parents and found that the first semester end date was not as important as the extra week of summer, when students were still going to camps and on vacations."

The Ankeny, Iowa, school district conducts a written, communitywide survey every 5 years to determine the public's wants and needs and to establish long-range plans. Other community agencies, such as the public library, municipal parks and recreation department, YMCA and YWCA, and local United Way also include questions about their services in the survey.

Superintendent Dr. Ben Norman says the survey, as well as focus groups that discuss and act on survey results, keep the school district up to date on demographic trends such as population and length of stay in town, specific information that is heavily used. "It helps us understand the overall community," he says. Survey results are reviewed, discussed, and prioritized by a Community Education Advisory Council. Its mission is to decide which issues are of most importance and how different agencies can work together to address them. Resource 3–7 gives a more detailed description of the survey program, which has resulted in more than 30 school programs and/or partnerships since its inception.

Open-Door Policy Debate

Although open-door policies are a standard way of promoting communication, administrators disagree on their effectiveness.

Superintendent Rednak believes in the open-door philosophy and promotes it among the principals he supervises. The advice he gives is that part of the school administrator's position is to give people an opportunity to express their feelings. "Any person can come to my office and talk to me one-on-one or call me with concerns at any time," he says.

He also advises that principals apply an extra dose of patience when talking with visitors. "If you come off as harsh and cold, that verifies the image in people's minds that school administrators are cold and uncaring."

Open-door policies are valuable, but they should not be absolute, answers Principal Michael Simkins of Los Osos, California. Administrators are too busy with the responsibilities of running a school to devote the amount of time to concerned parents and community members that they demand. An open-door policy carried to the extreme could lead administrators into a daily routine of doing little more than listening to people and finding solutions to their problems, he says.

"By the time someone leaves my office, for example, I've usually promised to do something to help them. This will take time and effort above and beyond my normal daily responsibilities," he says.

Simkins strikes a balance between administrative responsibilities and community relations by posting a sheet outside his office where visitors can leave contact information. This ensures that individuals who drop by when he is unavailable or in a meeting don't go away empty handed. "They can write their name, telephone number, and subject of discussion on the sheet, and I get back to them and address their concern," he says.

In addition, an automated telephone answering system helps Simkins' office staff focus on customer service by eliminating the number of distractions a visitor must endure. "It's frustrating to people when they're standing in the office and the secretary can't give attention to them because he or she is on the phone or has to interrupt a conversation to answer the telephone," he says.

The voice mail system allows the secretary to focus on issues at hand, without worrying about incoming calls.

CONCLUSION

It is not imperative that schools add programs designed specifically to fit type 2 involvement. It is only necessary that they give closer attention to the ways in which they already communicate—newsletters, conferences, handbooks, open forums, surveys, and press releases. Chief among the improvement strategies are the following:

- Listen to what people say.
- Respond to opinions and suggestions in a timely, thoughtful manner.
- Make the school and its staff accessible and approachable.
- Help staff to refine their communication skills.
- Have a communication plan for times of crisis.

In addition to using current communication methods, school leaders should also prepare themselves to take advantage of technology and the communication methods it presents: e-mail, World Wide Web sites, and video communication. These methods can make relaying information to and from both internal and external audiences faster and more convenient.

Resource 3–1

School Choice Fair

Fort Wayne Community Schools
Fort Wayne, Indiana

Issue addressed: Making parents and community members aware of the advantages and assets of individual schools
Agencies involved: School district, member schools
Type of community: Urban
Approximate student enrollment: 31,969
Start date: 1992

Program Description and Structure

School choice within and among public school districts and increasing enrollment at many private schools mean that all schools must take advantage of opportunities to actively promote their unique programs and curricula. The annual School Choice Fair in Fort Wayne, Indiana, provides an opportunity for all 51 district schools to do this. Last year more than 2,000 community members attended.

At the fair, which is held at the convention center, schools are arranged according to location so people know what feeder path their students will follow should they choose a particular elementary school. Parents, students, and community members are free to visit the exhibition areas, look at the advantages of each school, and ask questions of school representatives.

"Every school prepares handouts and some perform demonstrations," says district Communications Specialist Kelly L. Updike. "Most groups rally around their school colors or choose a theme. One school's theme was 'under construction' because it was in the midst of a three-year renovation project, and signs and barricades led parents through [the] dis-

play area." The fair also features information booths about the district's student services, security, special education, and career center programs. For a fee, educational vendors, including computer companies and textbook publishers, can display their wares and talk with participating parents and schools.

Since its inception, the fair has grown steadily. Attendance has doubled over past years and 100 percent of exit evaluations indicate approval and appreciation.

Planning Process

Preparation for the fair begins early. In November, principals meet in each of the six district zones to brainstorm pros and cons regarding the previous year's event. Updike handles the event's logistic arrangements, such as contracting for the facility, and communicates regularly with the schools to keep them abreast of planning progress.

She also prepares a 16- to 18-page directory of participating schools as a guide for fair attendees. This information booklet provides easy-to-read bullet-style lists of school programs, a district map, and a one-page matrix summarizing different features of each school. "Throughout the year, we also make the booklets available at the city visitor's bureau, send them to parents interested in the district, and mail them to all preschools," Updike says.

Planning for the fair is time consuming, but Updike says the following steps simplify the process:

- *Create a purpose.* Be able to answer the questions, "Why do we want people to come?" and "What do we want them to do?"

- *Identify a means to reach the target audience.* People will not attend if they don't know what is going on. Once you know your audience, choose the most effective ways to reach it.
- *Assess the resources.* "We make lists of what we can get free, what we will need to pay for, and who we can recruit to help. This year, for example, we asked the district Parent–Teacher Association council to serve as the event's host, greeting people at the door," says Updike.
- *Make sure everyone understands the event's goal.* Constant communication is the key to keeping staff members informed. "Pick different media to convey your message—memos, employee newsletters, meetings, even radio and television spots," she says.
- *Focus on the day's events.* Pay attention to details. Know who is responsible for what, and know what everybody is doing.
- *Communicate progress.* Updike meets regularly with principals and sends memos explaining what the district is doing and what staff members need to do.

Funding

Staging the fair is an expensive venture. Approximately $34,000 came from Updike's district fund used to promote racial balance. (The fair was established in 1992 to support a voluntary desegregation plan.) The lion's share of the budget, $18,000, was spent on the production of the information booklets. The other primary expenses were facility rental and publicity, at $5,000 and $10,000, respectively.

"The facility itself becomes expensive because we have to pay rental fees for the tables, chairs, and divider curtains we use," says Updike. "However, we never allocate a set amount for each aspect of the fair. Every year we modify the budget."

Participation and Publicity

Updike says the fair is an effective way for schools to tell their stories and to market both their facilities and the district as a whole. However, some schools hesitate to get involved because they feel there is no need to market themselves. "I remind administrators that the fair is a district activity [that] provides them the opportunity to talk to parents about the good things their schools are doing. This is positive marketing that reflects on the district," she says.

To publicize the event, Updike uses all media—school newsletters, on-site promotions, and radio and television spots. "People without children make up the majority of our population, so our advertising makes a point of inviting everyone, not just parents, to see the school choices in our district."

An Open House Week at all elementary schools follows the fair. During this time, parents can meet individually with principals to ask more pointed questions about enrollment and programs and to tour individual schools.

For more information about the School Choice Fair, contact Fort Wayne Community Schools, 1200 South Clinton Street, Fort Wayne, IN 46802; telephone (219) 425-7227.

Resource 3–2

Getting Ready for a Conference

Dear Parent or Guardian:

Your child's success in school is very important to all of us. By sharing our observations and insights, we can understand your child's strengths and how to best help him or her learn.

Will you please take the time to meet with me in your child's classroom? Please tell me what times and dates would be most convenient for you. (Please indicate in the space provided below the dates and times you prefer.)

Below are some questions that I may be asking you to talk about so I can better under-

stand your child and his or her style of learning. Attached to this sheet are some ideas for questions that you, as a parent or guardian, might want to ask me, your child's teacher.

Please read this sheet and return the top portion to me by _____
or feel free to call me at school _____
with the times you'll be available. I look forward to making this a happy and productive year for your child!

Sincerely,

_____

- -

Questions Teachers May Ask Parents or Guardians

1. What does your child like most about school?
2. What does your child think he or she is "good at doing"? Describe your child's hobbies or interests.
3. What types of things are difficult for your child to do?
4. What activities do you and your child enjoy doing together?
5. How does your child do homework? Where is it done?
6. Describe your child's friends. Are you satisfied with your child's choice of friends and activities?
7. Are there any attitudes or behaviors your child has toward school that you would like to see changed?
8. What can I do to support you at home in academic, social, or developmental areas in which you would like to see your child improve?
9. Are there any areas in which you would like more information about what your child is learning or how students are graded?
10. What do you hope your child learns this year? What are your dreams for his or her future?

Source: Reprinted from *Getting Ready for a Conference*, with permission of the Wisconsin Department of Public Instruction, John T. Benson, Superintendent.

Resource 3–3

School Conferences

Questions To Help Parents or Guardians at Conference Time

1. What is my child's class schedule?

2. What will my child be learning this year in reading? Math? Science? Social Studies?

3. Are children grouped in reading, math, or other subjects? What group is my child in, and how are children selected for each group?

4. Do you think my child is working up to his or her ability?

5. In what areas do you think my child is doing well?

6. In what subjects do you think my child needs improvement?

7. What are the most important things you think children in your classroom should learn? How can I help encourage this learning at home?

8. How is my child's work evaluated?

9. Can you show me examples of my child's work—classroom projects, tests, special assignments?

10. How much time should my child spend on homework? How can I help with homework?

11. What can you tell me about how my child seems to learn best? Is he or she a "hands-on" learner? Does he or she need to move around? Does he or she enjoy learning in a cooperative group or prefer working alone in a quiet environment?

12. How do your classroom strategies complement my child's style of learning?

13. How do you discipline students in your classroom?

14. Does my child get along with other children? With you?

15. In what other ways can I reinforce classroom learning at home or be informed about my child's progress in school? Are there opportunities for parents to be involved in classroom activities?

16. What special interest activities are available to encourage my child to learn?

Source: Reprinted from *School Conferences: Questions to Help Parents or Guardians at Conference Time*, with permission of the Wisconsin Department of Public Instruction, John T. Benson, Superintendent.

Resource 3–4

Elderclass

Beachwood Community Schools
Beachwood, Ohio

Issue addressed: Dealing with senior citizen dissociation from the school district and the possibility of losing their support for school bond initiatives
Agencies involved: School, senior citizens
Type of community: Suburban
Approximate student enrollment: 1,500
Start date: 1989

Program Description and Goals

Senior citizens typically are among the hardest individuals to reach when trying to generate support for schools because they no longer have children of school age and therefore have little vested interest in school issues or events. Elderclass, a program of the Beachwood Community Schools in Beachwood, Ohio, however, is reversing this trend.

The program was initiated by board member Saul Eisen in 1989 and offers senior citizens programs specifically tailored to their interests and needs. According to Communications Coordinator Lois Cooper, Eisen believed that after senior citizens were in the school, they would begin to understand that the taxes they pay to support the schools are well spent.

Benefits

Elderclass offers a number of benefits for senior citizens.

- *Monthly luncheons and lectures*. Elderclass organizes monthly luncheons catered by the school's vocational students, followed by programs and/or lectures on topics of interest to seniors, such as travel and grandparenting. Cooper says the events are well attended and reservations are required.
- *Computer courses*. For seniors who want to get in touch with technology, Elderclass offers two 8-week computer courses. The fist course covers the basics of computer vocabulary and operation; the second course explores more advanced computer uses, such as tracking and calculating taxes. Other computing lessons include word processing, e-mail, and what to look for when purchasing a computer. Interest in the classes has been so high, says Cooper, that additional courses have been added.
- *Free admission to school events*. One of the first steps taken by the Beachwood City School Board was to eliminate admission fees to some school events for persons 50 years of age or older.
- *Physical fitness facilities*. For $25 a year, senior citizens and other residents can use the building's exercise equipment and indoor track.

Governing Committee and Publicity

The Elderclass governing committee organized itself when several participants volunteered to identify the topics of most interest. "The program's coordinator became a liaison to the superintendent and school board to present the committee's ideas for approval," says Cooper. "If [an idea is] approved, we iron out the details with principals at individual schools."

Articles in the school district newsletter inform seniors about Elderclass and the opportunities available. Cooper says every time she runs an article, people ask to be added to the program's mailing list.

Costs

The school board pays an annual $5,400 fee for the program's part-time coordinator/consultant. Other program elements are coordinated by school district employees and students. The luncheons, for example, are held in a private dining room adjacent to the high school cafeteria and are catered by vocational education students studying food management and preparation. Guests are charged $4 for the meal.

A full-time teacher, who receives a stipend for after-school time, oversees and attends all computer courses. However, seventh- and eighth-grade students interested in computers actually present the classes. The teacher's stipend is covered by the $24 course registration fee.

Program Consultant Mort Biel says teachers are very willing to volunteer their time for one-time-only Elderclass sessions such as a pottery class or lessons on how to make tie-dyed T-shirts.

Results

Interest in the program, especially the computer courses, has grown over the years. More than 150 people registered for the first luncheon, and classes are almost always full. Both Cooper and Biel say the school board is supportive and that their concern for senior citizens has been returned to them in the form of support for school bond issues.

"This program evolved with the idea that the only time the school district comes to senior citizens is when it needs a tax levy or bond issue approved," says Biel. "This is an attempt to get seniors into the schools and show them that the school system cares about them, and not just their money."

For more information about the Elderclass program, contact Beachwood Public Schools, 24601 Fairmount Boulevard, Beachwood, OH 44122; telephone (216) 831-2080.

Resource 3–5

Discover the Excellence

Canandaigua City School District
Canandaigua, New York

Issue addressed: Familiarizing new students and parents with the school in a nonthreatening way
Agencies involved: School district, community library
Type of community: Small city
Approximate student enrollment: 4,250
Start date: 1994

Program Description

To ease the transition to a new school, the Canandaigua City Schools in Canandaigua, New York, developed a 20-minute orientation videotape for parents and students new to the district's primary school. The video presentation, "Discover the Excellence," is narrated by two third-grade students. This videotape outlines school rules and practices and is available for checkout at the local library.

The project won a 1995 Pinnacle Award for excellence in education in the board and district operations category.

Community Relations Coordinator Andrew Thomas says the videotape provides parents and children, whether new kindergarteners or transfer students, with a friendly, nonthreatening orientation session that they can review and discuss at home.

"We believe that if parents and students watch together in the comfort of their own living rooms, students will feel a lot better about coming to school on their first day," says Thomas.

Benefits

The primary benefit of the videotape is that it provides another vehicle for explaining school

policies and practices. The school handbook includes the same information, says Thomas, but parents don't always realize which information in it is most important.

"And some information that's important when people first come to the school is not part of the handbook," he says. "They want to know what the various programs are like, what the people look like, where the cafeteria is in relation to the student's room, that sort of thing. Parents can get [some information] from a map, but it's tougher to visualize. The video shows actual parents and students doing things."

One of the practices depicted in the videotape is the district's rotating, 6-day schedule of "specials." "We're always questioned about that, so we made sure it was addressed in the video," says Thomas.

The video presentation format also contributes to students' sense of security. "The tape isn't always slick, but you don't want slickness. You want something that speaks the truth and appeals to parents and to their children," he says. "When the video tour guides say, 'Let's go visit the classroom,' it's friendly [and] engaging, and the students watching feel like they're being spoken to personally, because students like themselves are leading the tour. This is far more appealing than if the tape featured an administrator talking about policies."

Production Process

The idea for the videotape was conceived by a school board subcommittee focused on community relations. It is patterned after a tourism video presentation that featured a cab driver narrating a tour of the city with the camera as the passenger. It gives viewers a first-person look at the school building's layout and explains common rules and procedures. Producing the videotape involved several subcommittee members, including school board members, students and staff, and Thomas, who has background in television production.

Two third-grade students served as tour guides. As they walked through the school, they described where they were and explained rules and procedures. When all video footage was collected, the tape was professionally edited. The entire production process took about 1 year, at a cost of approximately $1,000; most of the cost was due to the editing process.

Although videotape has proved to be an informative and convenient way to deliver information, Thomas cites two specific problems with the medium.

1. *Accepting mediocre quality.* "When you're making a video, you need to be as good as you can be. Poorly done video looks really bad. And people are used to seeing high-quality video on television and in movies," he says. Thomas says that parents don't expect the school district to be Steven Spielberg. If schools want people to respond to tapes, however, they "can't look like a home video."

2. *Using the video too long.* Clothing, hairstyles, furniture, and language often give away the year of production and can actually distract from the videotape's message if it is used too long, says Thomas. "We will need to update the tape in a few years so it doesn't start to look dated, and [we will need] to make sure the policies are up to date. We're expecting each video to have a shelf life of about four to five years."

For more information about Discover the Excellence, contact the Canandaigua City Schools, 143 North Pearl Street, Canandaigua, NY, 14424; telephone (716) 396-3714.

Resource 3-6

Neighborhood Meetings

Fort Plain Central School District
Fort Plain, New York

Issue addressed: Nurturing support for the school district and generating feedback about school issues and programs
Agencies involved: School, Parent–Teacher Organization
Type of community: Rural
Approximate student enrollment: 1,100
Start date: 1992

Program Description

To maintain awareness of school activities, Superintendent and High School Principal John Metallo conducts regular, informational meetings for parents and community residents in the heart of their comfort zones—their homes. Members of the Fort Plain Central School District's Parent–Teacher Organization in Fort Plain, New York, organize the gatherings, where attendees can talk with school staff and parents about specific issues and/or concerns.

"We wanted to foster support for our school programs and, at the same time, generate input from parents and community members," says Metallo. "The neighborhood meeting idea is an effective way to do this."

The meetings have been particularly effective in the dissemination of program-specific information. Past topics have included state financial aid and other resources, student grouping, ability tracking, cooperative learning, services available through the school, and the high school's reading lists, as well as how parents can contact teachers and how students can conduct college searches.

Rumor control is an added benefit of the meetings, says Metalo. "Even when people don't truly know how things work, they think they do. These meetings give us a chance to tell people how the school district actually does things."

Preparation and Participation

The team of school representatives varies from one meeting to the next. Metallo typically attends, as does the district's other principal; others including teachers, guidance counselors, and school nurses participate as relevant topics are discussed. These participants give short overviews of current events in their respective areas at the meeting's start. Audience questions follow.

Metallo estimates that 10–40 people attend each of the six to eight meetings each year. Additional meetings are held as situations warrant. "The most important factor in getting maximum participation is that we conduct meetings when the community wants us to," he says.

Volunteer hosts and hostesses, who are solicited by the Parent–Teacher Association, prepare refreshments and develop the guest list. They may invite everyone from the neighborhood, or the meeting may be organized only for parents who have children of a certain age.

The home atmosphere, says Metallo, improves attendance and participation. "The informal atmosphere of a neighbor's home is attractive to parents and residents, especially those who are uncomfortable in the school's formal setting. People are less intimidated by school staff and more at ease with themselves," he says.

Although the neighborhood meeting is a simple idea, it is not one Metallo will easily give up. "The meetings are well attended and very positive. Participants all express interest in the opportunity to do it again," he says.

For more information, contact the Fort Plain Central School District, Fort Plain, NY, telephone (518) 993-2123.

Resource 3–7

Charrette—A Community Survey

Ankeny Community Schools
Ankeny, Iowa

Issues addressed: Dealing with the need for cooperative long-range planning between the school district and other community agencies
Agencies involved: School district, Chamber of Commerce, nonprofit organizations, city government, parks and recreation, library, churches
Type of community: Suburban
Approximate student enrollment: 5,230
Start date: 1977

Program Description

Since 1977, the Ankeny, Iowa, school district, with cooperation from other municipal agencies, has organized a survey called Charrette, to find out what residents want for the community in future years. The French term means "bringing things together," according to Superintendent Ben Norman. He says the survey helps the district plan for the future, as well as providing demographic information such as population and length of stay in town.

To date, Charrette has been responsible for the creation of more than 20 programs, including the Juvenile Justice Council, citizens' planning conferences, a community improvement task force, a sports complex, a parenting task force, a senior citizen transportation service, and a youth activities task force.

Various community groups, including the city, the library, the United Way, and the YMCA and YWCA participate in the survey by adding questions related to their services and plans. The 8- to 10-page survey then is randomly distributed to 1,200 residents. A community advisory council, also organized by

the school district, reviews survey results with a focus group during a weekend retreat.

Survey and Focus Groups

Boy Scout volunteers distribute and pick up survey packets, which include the survey, a cover letter signed by the school superintendent and the city major describing the survey's purpose, and an envelope for returning the survey. Residents also receive directions for completing the survey.

The advisory council plans a weekend retreat with 50–60 citizens representing the schools, residents of the city and outlying areas, senior citizens, students, and organizations such as the Lions Club and Kiwanis Club. Norman also invites the city manager, chief of police, state legislators, and local politicians. The 3-day retreats usually are held at a Boy Scout or church camp because those facilities are large and inexpensive. Five or six key issues identified in the surveys are discussed.

"Participants begin by developing project ideas and identifying issues that they feel need to be addressed in the future," says Norman. "They break into small discussion groups, brainstorm ways to address the extensive list of issues, and report their ideas to the full group. I ask a number of experts, from legislators to police officers, to speak on various topics. Then we conduct a forum in which group members talk with the experts about the issues."

By the end of the retreat, participants commit themselves to serve on one of three or four

Courtesy of Ankeny Community School District, Ankeny, Iowa.

Resource 3–7 continued

committees devoted to a key issue. "The committees meet, appoint a chairperson, and recruit others to serve until the problem is solved and the committee is dropped," says Norman.

Participation and Cost

Because the Charrette survey is personally delivered and picked up, the recipient's only obligation is to complete it. However, involvement in committee work depends on the ability to show results. "The first time we did this, we had trouble encouraging people to make the commitment," says Norman. "We kept telling [participants] that their time and effort would be worthwhile. And after the first focus group 'cycle,' it was easier because people could see our success."

The cost for printing the Charrette survey is minimal compared with the expense of renting a retreat facility and paying for meals. However, most groups who send representatives to the retreat, such as the Rotary Club and Lions Club, fund their people. Participants who are not financially supported by an organization receive a "scholarship by the school district."

Recent Success

The school district recently formed a partnership with the YMCA for construction and use of a new swimming pool facility on school grounds. They raised $500,000 toward an endowment fund to purchase materials that keep the facility up to date, so the financial burden never falls back on the taxpayers beyond the cost of regular school bond issues.

The partnership provides for school district residents to become members of the YMCA at a reduced fee, and a formal contract outlines each party's responsibilities regarding the pool. Norman says the school board president and the YMCA executive director meet bimonthly to discuss scheduling, so that the school is able to conduct physical education classes at one end of the pool while the senior citizens do aqua-aerobics at the other end.

Sample Materials

On the following pages are samples of the materials used in a Charrette survey.

For more information about the Charrette program, contact Ankeny Community Schools, 306 Southwest School Street, P.O. Box 189, Ankeny, IA 50021-0819; telephone (515) 965-9600.

1995 Ankeny Community Betterment Survey

Directions: Please read each question below, then answer by selecting one of the response choices listed. Place the number associated with your response choice in the blank to the left of each question.

____1. How long have you lived within the Ankeny Community School District?

  1. 0–2 years   2. 2–5 years   3. 5–10 years   4. Over 10 years

____2. How long do you anticipate living in this community?

  1. 0–2 years   2. 2–5 years   3. 5–10 years   4. Over 10 years

____3. From which source do you best receive community information? Select only ONE.

  1. Ankeny Press Citizen-Crier   4. Hawkline (school newspaper)
  2. Des Moines Register Neighbors   5. Others (specify) _____
  3. KJJY radio (92.5 FM)

____4. Has anyone in your household ever attended an adult education class in Ankeny?

  1. Yes   2. No

____5. Has anyone in your household ever participated in a program sponsored by the Ankeny Parks and Recreation Department?

  1. Yes   2. No

____6. Does anyone in your household belong to a local civic or community service organization?

  1. Yes   2. No

____7. Which weekday evening (5:00 to 10:00 PM) is best for you to attend classes, programs, or activities? Select only ONE.

  1. Monday   2. Tuesday   3. Wednesday   4. Thursday

____8. Would you favor after-school or evening "enrichment classes" (e.g., academic, business, industrial arts, hobby offerings) to be offered to high school students on a no-credit basis?

  1. Yes   2. No   3. Don't know

____9. Would you favor after-school or evening "enrichment classes" (e.g., academic, business, industrial arts, hobby offerings) to be offered to middle school students?

  1. Yes   2. No   3. Don't know

____10. Would you favor after-school or evening "enrichment classes" to be offered to grades 4 and 5?

  1. Yes   2. No   3. Don't know

____11. Would you like to take a high school course during the regular school day?

  1. Yes   2. No   3. No, but another adult in my household probably would

11a. If so, what course(s) _____

11b. Would you want high school or college credit for this course? Circle Yes or No.

  1. Yes   2. No.

Resource 3–7 continued

____12. Do you pay to send your youngster(s), age 5–12, to *after*-school child care?

     1. Yes   2. No   3. Not applicable in my household

____13. Do you pay to send your youngster(s), age 5–12, to *before*-school child care?

     1. Yes   2. No   3. Not applicable to my household

____14. Is any member of your household currently certified in first aid or CPR?

     1. Yes   2. No

15. Within the last year, have you or a member of your household been involved in the following? Place a (✓) in the blank to the left of the item, checking ALL that apply.

     ____a. Attended a city council or school board meeting
     ____b. Attended a meeting, concert, or play at school
     ____c. Attended a meeting, seminar, cultural event, or class at Des Moines Area Community College
     ____d. Actively participated in a church organization or group
     ____e. Utilized your Kirkendall Library card
     ____f. Attended a nonschool, nonathletic event scheduled in a school building

____16. Are you a registered voter?

     1. Yes   2. No

____17. Do you like to keep Sunday free for worship or church-related activity?

     1. Yes   2. No

____18. Do you like to keep Wednesday evening free for church-related activity?

     1. Yes   2. No

____19. Did you know that school facilities are generally available at no charge for "local community service" needs?

     1. Yes   2. No

____20. Are you aware that the Ankeny Community Education Advisory Council exists to address total community needs?

     1. Yes   2. No

____21. Do you support continuation of Ankeny Summerfest?

     1. Yes   2. No   3. No opinion

____22. Child safety procedures are efficiently managed by Ankeny police.

     1. Agree   2. Disagree   3. No strong opinion

____23. Ankeny schools provide appropriate levels of child safety information.

     1. Agree   2. Disagree   3. No strong opinion

____24. Do you have comments about costs or availability of the city or school facilities in Ankeny?

     1. Yes   2. No   3. Comments_____

_____25. Do you have any comments about school curriculum?

    1. Yes   2. No   3. Comments_____

_____

_____26. Do you have any comments about student discipline?

    1. Yes   2. No   3. Comments_____

_____

_____27. Do you have any comments about quality of education in Ankeny?

    1. Yes   2. No   3. Comments_____

_____

_____28. Do you have any comments about class size?

    1. Yes   2. No   3. Comments_____

_____

29. Select THREE of the following choices which, in your opinion, are of the greatest concern to our Ankeny community. Place a check (✓) in the blank to the left of the choice.

    _____a. Substance abuse   _____f. Infant and child care

    _____b. Crime/public safety   _____g. Available, affordable housing

    _____c. Crime (juvenile)   _____h. Unemployment/underemployment

    _____d. Economic growth   _____i. Youth programs

    _____e. Environmental issues, pollution

30. Please describe or clarify your top choice(s) of concern in item 29.

_____

_____

31. List any other concern or need for improvement in the Ankeny community.

_____

_____

32. List the reason(s) why, in your opinion, Ankeny is a good community in which to live.

_____

_____

_____33. Do you have any comments about local problems or possible solutions regarding the abuse of alcohol or drugs?

    1. Yes   2. No   3. Comments_____

_____

_____34. What is your age?

    1. 18–24 years   4. 46–54 years

    2. 26–35 years   5. 55–65 years

    3. 36–45 years   6. Over 65

_____35. What is your sex?

    1. Female   2. Male

Resource 3–7 continued

____36. In which Ankeny elementary school attendance area do you reside?

    1. East   5. Southeast
    2. Northeast   6. Terrace
    3. Northwest   7. Westwood
    4. Rural (all dwelling outside Ankeny city limits)

If you responded that you reside in a rural area, please continue with item 37. If you gave any other response, please go to item 46.

____37. Are you aware that city leisure services offered by the Ankeny schools are available to you under the same conditions as to residents within the Ankeny city limits?

    1. Yes   2. No

____38. Have you or has any member of your family attended an adult education class or any activity offered in and/or by the Ankeny schools?

    1. Yes   2. No

____39. Do you do most of your grocery shopping in Ankeny?

    1. Yes   2. No

____40. Which of the following do you most often purchase in Ankeny? Please select only ONE.

    1. Car or truck fuel   4. Clothing
    2. Household goods   5. Home repair or maintenance items
    3. Meals (fast-food or other)   6. Entertainment facilities or items

____41. Do you use the Kirkendall Public Library?

    1. Yes   2. No

____42. Do you have a Kirkendall library card?

    1. Yes   2. No

____43. Do you belong to the Ankeny Family YMCA?

    1. Yes   2. No

____44. Do you use any services or programs offered by the Ankeny Family YMCA?

    1. Yes   2. No

____45. Are you aware that membership in the Ankeny Family YMCA is available to you at the same cost as that offered to residents within the Ankeny city limits?

    1. Yes   2. No

____46. What is your marital status? Select only ONE.

    1. Never married   4. Divorced
    2. Married (1st marriage)   5. Separated
    3. Remarried   6. Widow(er)

____47. Are you employed?

1. No, do not desire employment at this time
2. No, but desire employment
3. Yes, part time
4. Yes, full time

____48. What city is nearest your place of employment?

1. None (not employed)
2. Ankeny
3. Des Moines

4. Ames
5. West Des Moines
6. Other (specify)_____

____49. Have you actively pursued employment closer to home?

1. Yes   2. No

____50. Is your spouse employed?

1. No spouse
2. No, does not desire employment
3. No, but desires employment

4. Yes, part time
5. Yes, full time

____51. What is the number of people residing in your household? (Please write the number.)

____52. Total annual household income:

1. $0–10,000
2. $10–15,000
3. $15–20,000
4. $20–30,000

5. $30–40,000
6. $40–50,000
7. $50–75,000
8. Over $75,000

Resource 3–7 continued

1995 Ankeny Area Chamber of Commerce Section

Directions: Please read each question below, then answer by selecting one of the response choices listed. Place the number associated with your response choice in the blank to the left of each question.

1. Please rank the factors that influence you most to shop in Ankeny in order of importance with 1 being most important and 5 least important.

    ____a. Cost   ____d. Selection
    ____b. Convenience   ____e. Service
    ____c. Quality of product

____2. Which form of advertising do you respond to most often? Select only ONE.

    Newspaper   2. Television
    1a. Ankeny Today Advertiser   3. Radio
    1b. Ankeny Press Citizen   4. Coupons
    1c. Ankeny Today
    1d. Des Moines Register

____3. Have you used The Source telephone information system?

    1. Yes   3. No, but plan to use it soon
    2. No   4. No, never heard of it

____4. If you answered yes to item 3, did you find it helpful?

    1. Yes   2. No

____5. If you answered yes to item 3, do you plan to use it again?

    1. Yes   2. No

____6. Would you be more likely to shop in Ankeny if businesses were open at least one evening during the week?

    1. Yes   2. No   3. No difference

____7. If you answered yes to item 6, which ONE evening of the week would your household most value having Ankeny businesses open?

    1. Monday   5. Friday
    2. Tuesday   6. Saturday
    3. Wednesday   7. Sunday
    4. Thursday

____8. Overall, are you satisfied with the products and services available in Ankeny?

    1. Yes   2. No   3. Somewhat

____9. Do you feel you are familiar with the businesses and products available in Ankeny?

    1. Yes   2. No   3. Somewhat

1995 Kirkendall Public Library Section

Directions for Parts A, B, C, and D: For Parts A, B, C, and D below, indicate each item or program that someone from your household has used within the last year at the library. Place a check (✓) in the blank to the left of each appropriate item. CHECK ALL THAT APPLY.

A. Collections

____1. Books
____2. Magazines
____3. Foreign language tapes
____4. College catalogues
____5. Genealogical materials
____6. Career information

____ 7. Pamphlets
____ 8. Reference materials
____ 9. Paperback books
____10. Travel brochures
____11. Telephone books
____12. Census materials

____13. Audiocassettes
____14. Newspapers
____15. Large-print books
____16. Cassette books
____17. Videocassettes
____18. Maps

B. Equipment

____19. 16-mm projectors
____20. Cassette players/recorders
____21. Recording equipment
____22. Videocassette players

____23. Record player
____24. Screens
____25. Opaque projectors
____26. Overhead projectors

____27. Carousel slide projectors
____28. Typewriters
____29. Lectern

C. Programs

____30. Summer reading program
____31. Childrens' crafts
____32. Preschool story hours

____33. "Specials" for children
____34. Book discussion groups

____35. Young adult programs
____36. Adult programs

D. Services

____37. Telephone reference (965-6460)
____38. Dial-a-story (965-6462)
____39. Copy machine
____40. Home delivery for shut ins
____41. Meeting room

____42. Film service (16-mm)
____43. Interlibrary loan
____44. Book drop (24 hours)
____45. Reading lists
____46. In-house computers
____47. In-house typewriters
____48. Notary service

____49. Art exhibits
____50. City/county directories
____51. Guided tours
____52. Laminating
____53. Zip code book
____54. Tax forms

Directions for Parts E and F: For Parts E and F, select from the list of choices the THREE items in each section that you feel are the most important Kirkendall services. In the blank at the left of the choices, place a 1 for the *most important* item, a 2 for the *second most important* item, and a 3 for the *third most important* item.

E. Existing Kirkendall services (Select THREE items and rank them.)

____55. Reference (phone and in-house)
____56. Large-print books
____57. Telephone books
____58. Typewriters (in-house/ checkout)

____59. Children's programs
____60. Books on tape
____61. Magazines
____62. Equipment that may circulate

____63. Adult programs
____64. In-house computer
____65. Home delivery

Resource 3–7 continued

F.   New service possibilities (Select THREE items and rank them.)

____66. Enlarged book collection
____67. (More) Large-print books
____68. (More) Magazines (Please suggest) _____
____69. (More) Iowa books and local history area
____70. (More) Paperback books

____71. (More) Maps
____72. (More) Sheet music
____73. Enlarged business collection/business area
____74. Extended hours
____75. Des Moines Register on microfilm

____76. Genealogy area
____77. CD ROM collection
____78. (More) Out-of-town newspapers (Please suggest) _____
_____
_____

Directions: Please read each question below, then answer by selecting one of the response choices. Place the number associated with your response choice in the blank to the left of each question.

____79. Do you use the other urban libraries (Des Moines, Urbandale, West Des Moines)?
    1. Often   2. Sometimes   3. Seldom   4. Never

____80. Would you be willing to fund computer linkup with other area libraries for collection access?

1995 Parks and Recreation Section

Directions: Please read each question below, then answer by selecting one of the response choices listed. Place the number associated with your response choice in the blank to the left of each question.

____1. Within the past year, how often have you or any member of your family utilized the parks and recreation facilities in Ankeny?

    1. 1–6 times   2. 7–12 times   3. More than 12 times   4. Not at all

____2. Using Ankeny Boulevard and First Street as dividing lines, within which quadrant do you live?

    1. Northwest   2. Northeast   3. Southwest   4. Southeast   5. Rural

3. During the past year, have you or your family utilized any of the following park and recreation facilities provided by the city of Ankeny? To the left of each facility, please rate its importance to you: **1 = Low** to **5 = High**. To the right of each facility, please indicate your level of satisfaction with each facility:
**5 = Very satisfied   4 = Somewhat satisfied   3 = Moderately satisfied
2 = Somewhat dissatisfied   1 = Very dissatisfied**

Importance	Facilities	Satisfaction	Importance	Facilities	Satisfaction
____a.	Community/senior center	____	____n.	Platform tennis courts	____
____b.	Lakeside Center	____	____o.	Basketball courts	____
____c.	Family picnic area	____	____p.	Handball courts	____
____d.	Open picnic shelters	____	____q.	Shuffleboard courts	____
____e.	Playgrounds	____	____r.	Sand volleyball courts	____
____f.	Softball fields	____	____s.	Swimming pool	____
____g.	Soccer fields	____	____t.	Wading pool	____
____h.	Baseball fields	____	____u.	Otter Creek Golf Course	____
____i.	Football fields	____	____v.	Driving range	____
____j.	Batting cages	____	____w.	Disc golf course	____
____k.	Bicycle trail	____	____x.	Open green spaces	____
____l.	Walking trail	____	____y.	Wildlife/natural area	____
____m.	Tennis courts	____			

4. Do you think the city of Ankeny needs the following new facilities incorporated into its new or existing parks? To the left of each facility, please rate its importance to you: 1 = Low to 5 = High.

Importance	Facilities	Importance	Facilities
_____a.	Rollerblade trail	_____l.	Nature study areas
_____b.	Go-cart track	_____m.	Water slides
_____c.	Miniature golf	_____n.	Remote car track
_____d.	BMX bike trails	_____o.	Snow sledding hill
_____e.	Horseback riding	_____p.	Outdoor ice hockey
_____f.	Wildlife habitat	_____q.	Archery
_____g.	Indoor roller skating	_____r.	Paddle boating
_____h.	Practice tennis wall	_____s.	Canoeing
_____i	Compact fitness station	_____t.	Obstacle course
_____j.	Cross-country skiing	_____u.	Linear parks (along streams)
_____k.	New parks		

____5. How important would it be to you or your family to link Ankeny to the Saylorville and surrounding bike trails? Indicate importance by rating: 1 = Low to 5 = High.

Resource 3–7 continued

6. Please identify by placing a check (✓) in the blank to the left of the parks you or your family have visited during the past year. Mark ALL that apply.

_____a. Crestbruck Park	_____h. Village Park
_____b. Otter Creek Park	_____i. Sunset Park
_____c. Westwood Park	_____j. Otter Creek Golf Course
_____d. Westside Park	_____k. Haubert Park
_____e. Hawkeye Sports Complex	_____l. Sunrise Park
_____f. Greentree Park	_____m. Wagner Park
_____g. Heritage Park	_____n. Hawkeye Park

____7. Overall, how satisified are you with the quality of park services and facilities provided by the city of Ankeny?

5 = Very satisfied   4 = Somewhat satisfied   3 = Moderately satisfied
2 = Somewhat dissatisfied   1 = Very dissatisfied

Comments:_____

_____

____8. In the past year, how many youth, adult, or senior citizen programs/activities provided by the Leisure Services Department have you or your family participated in?

1 = 11 or more   2 = 8–10   3 = 5–7   4 = 3–4   5 = 1–2   6 = None

9. What are the top THREE sources of information you have used to gain knowledge about leisure services activities? Place a check (✓) in the blank to the left of your THREE choices.

_____a. Ankeny newspapers	_____e. Fliers sent through schools
_____b. Radio	_____f. Mailings
_____c. Hawkline	_____g. Posters in businesses
_____d. Summer brochure	_____h. Other (specify)_____

___10. During the past year, how many times have you or your family visited the Ankeny Municipal Pool?

1 = 20 or more   2 = 16–20   3 = 11–15   4 = 6–10   5 = 1–5   6 = None

11. The city of Ankeny will be building a new aquatic facility in the near future. Please indicate the importance of pool facilities to you by rating each of the following pool facility options: 1 = Low to 5 = High.

_____a. Water slide	_____f. Concessions
_____b. Sand volleyball court	_____g. Playground equipment
_____c. Zero-depth entry	_____h. Diving board
_____d. Sunbathing area	_____i. Heated pool water
_____e. Lap swimming lanes	_____j. Other (specify)_____

___12. Are you aware that the city of Ankeny has a rental facility, Community/Senior Center located on SW 3rd Street, that is available for private or community functions?

1. Yes   2. No

___13. Please indicate the importance of community rental facilities to you by rating 1 = Low to 5 = High.

___14. Overall, how satisfied are you and your family with the quality of programs you receive from the Leisure Services Department?

5 = Very satisfied   4 = Somewhat satisfied   3 = Moderately satisfied
2 = Somewhat dissatisfied   1 = Very dissatisfied

15. Please list any recreation programs that you or your family would like to see offered through the city of Ankeny Leisure Sevices Department _____

_____

_____

16. General comments about this section: _____

_____

_____

_____

_____

Resource 3–7 continued

1995 Senior Citizen Inquiry Section

Directions: Please read each question below, then answer by placing a check (✓) in the blank to the left of your response choice.

1. Does a member of your family use adult day care?

    ____Yes   ____No

2. Would a family member attend adult day care if available in Ankeny?

    ____Yes   ____No

3. Do you see barriers for adult day care?

    ____Yes   ____No

    If your response is yes, please list: _____

4. Would a member of your family use a congregate meal location?

    ____Yes   ____No

5. Would a member of your family use a transportation service?

    ____Yes   ____No

6. Would a member of your family benefit from health screens such as blood pressure checks or nutrition advice?

    ____Yes   ____No

7. What can be offered to fit your family's future needs?

    _____

    _____

    _____

    _____

    _____

    _____

8. Would you be willing to serve on a senior citizen's advisory board?

    _____

9. Your comments: _____

    _____

    _____

    _____

    _____

    _____

    _____

    _____

    _____

1995 United Way Section

Directions: Below is a list of services. Please answer the following three questions about each listed service by placing a check (✓) in the appropriate column if your response is **Yes**.

1. Are you aware of this service? (Check column 1 if your response is Yes.)

2. Do you know how to contact this service? (Check column 2 if your response is Yes.)

3. Have you used this service? (Check column 3 if your response is Yes.)

	Question 1 Aware	Question 2 Contact	Question 3 Used
a. TAKE: The Ankeny Clothing Exchange	____	____	____
b. Neveln Community Resource Center	____	____	____
c. ASAP: Ankeny Substance Abuse Project	____	____	____
d. Ankeny Family Advocacy Project	____	____	____
e. The Source: Phone Help Line	____	____	____
f. United Way Ankeny Service Center	____	____	____
g. Ankeny Counseling Services	____	____	____
h. Alcoholics Anonymous	____	____	____
i. Alanon	____	____	____
j. Alateen	____	____	____
k. Hospice	____	____	____
l. 911 emergency number	____	____	____
m. First Call for Help (Information/Referral Phone)	____	____	____
n. Elderly transportation	____	____	____
o. Volunteer center	____	____	____
p. Retired Senior Volunteer Program	____	____	____

Directions: Please answer each question below by placing a check (✓) in the blank to the left of your response choice.

4. Not including religious organizations, have you contributed to any charitable, nonprofit, or fund-raising organizations within the past 12 months?

____Yes   ____No

5. Do you or does any member of your family currently contribute time as a volunteer?

____Yes   ____No

6. Have you contributed to the United Way in the past 12 months?

____Yes   ____No

7. Are you aware that the following activities are currently available at the Neveln Community Resource Center? If your response is **Yes**, place a check (✓) on the line to the left of the activity. Check ALL that apply.

_____a.	Friends of the Arts	_____e.	Food pantry
_____b.	Ankeny Area Historical Society	_____f.	Exercise classes
_____c.	Computer user group	_____g.	Ankeny Connection
_____d.	TAKE (clothing program)		

8. Place a check (✓) in the blank to the left of additional activities you would like included at the Neveln Community Resource Center. Check ALL that apply.

_____a.	Card clubs	_____d.	Other (Please list) _____
_____b.	Youth or teen center		_____
_____c.	Congregate meal site for seniors		_____

Resource 3–7 continued

1995 Otter Creek Recreation Complex Section

Directions: Below is a list of facilities at our Otter Creek Recreation Complex. Please answer the following two questions about each listed service by placing a check (✓) in the appropriate column if your response is **Yes**.

1. Are you aware of this facility? (Check column 1 if your response is Yes.)

2. Will a member of your family use this facility? (Check column 2 if your response is Yes.)

	Question 1 **Aware**	**Question 2** **Use**
a. Sand playground	____	____
b. Driving range	____	____
c. Otter Creek Golf Course	____	____
d. Picnic and shelter area	____	____
e. Platform tennis court	____	____
f. Facility rental	____	____

3. Does anyone in your family play golf?   ____Yes   ____No

4. Do you have any constructive comments or suggested improvements regarding the Otter Creek Recreation Complex?

_____

_____

_____

_____

1995 Ankeny Family YMCA Section

Directions: Please read each question below, then answer by selecting one of the responses choices listed. Place a check (✓) in the blank to the left of your response choice for each question.

1. Do you currently participate in any **structured** recreation, sports, or exercise program?

    ____Yes   ____No

2. If you answered **Yes** to question 1, who sponsors the activity? Place a check (✓) in the blank to the left of ALL that apply.

    _____a. City Park and Recreation Dept.   _____e. Private health club
    _____b. YMCA   _____f. Company
    _____c. Church   _____g. Other (specify) _____
    _____d. Community education   _____

3. If you answered **Yes** to question 1, in what type of activity do you participate? Place a check (✓) in the blank to the left of ALL that apply.

    _____a. Team sport league   _____e. Exercise classes (land or water)
    _____b. Running/jogging   _____f. Weight lifting
    _____c. Bicycling   _____g. Martial arts classes
    _____d. Swimming   _____h. Other (specify)_____

4. What new recreation or sports opportunities would you like to see offered in the Ankeny community?

    _____

    _____

5. Do you or does any member of your family belong to a private, public, or nonprofit recreation organization?

    ____Yes   ____No

If you answered **Yes** to question 5, please answer questions 6 and 7. If you answered **No** to question 5, go to question 8.

6. If you answered Yes to question 5, place a check (✓) in the blank to the left of the organization(s) to which you belong. Check ALL that apply.

    _____a. Health club   _____d. YMCA
    _____b. Country club   _____e. Other (specify)_____
    _____c. Sport specialty club (e.g., martial arts)

7. If you or any member of your family belong to the YMCA, which type of membership do you have? Place a check (✓) in the blank to the left of your membership type.

    _____a. Adult   _____d. Single-parent family
    _____b. Youth   _____e. Senior citizen
    _____c. Family   _____f. Citywide (use of all YMCAs in
                                                                 Des Moines)

8. In what population group should the YMCA expand programming? Check ALL that apply.

    _____a. Infants (6–12 months)   _____f. High school (grades 10–12 years)
    _____b. Toddlers (13–24 months)   _____g. Adult-male (18–54 years)
    _____c. Preschool (3–5 years)   _____h. Adult-female (18–54 years)
    _____d. School age (grade K–5)   _____i. Senior citizens (over 55 years)
    _____e. Junior age (grades 6–9)   _____j. Persons with disabilities

Resource 3–7 continued

9. Of the following emerging community needs, which ones do you feel the YMCA should be addressing? Check ALL that apply.

_____a. Preschool child care   _____f. Expanded physical fitness program
_____b. School-age child care   _____g. Adult health education courses
_____c. Youth sports   _____h. Other (specify)_____
_____d. Adult sports   _____
_____e. Program for senior citizens   _____

Courtesy of Ankeny Community School District, Ankeny, Iowa.

CHAPTER 4

Type 3 Involvement: Volunteerism

To promote type 3 involvement, school leaders should recruit and organize parent help and support.

Volunteer programs are a cost-efficient way to expand the range of programs offered at a school, but involving parents and community residents in these programs is often difficult. Individuals have little time available for volunteer activities; those who do have time are often not reached by the school's recruitment efforts. Other potential volunteers avoid involvement because they fear being asked to perform tasks for which they are not trained.

A thoughtfully planned volunteer program and organized recruitment, screening, and supervision processes can help solve these problems. This chapter focuses on how to establish such a program, including the following components:

- outreach and publicity
- screening volunteers
- assigning and training volunteers
- evaluating volunteers and program

STRATEGIES

Outreach and Publicity

The ideal mix of program publicity methods will alert all residents, parents and nonparents alike, about volunteer opportunities in school. Joyce A. Housman, coordinator of the New Hyde Park–Garden City Park Volunteer Assistance Program at the public school district in New Hyde Park, New York, says her district's volunteer program started with a few small advertisements in the newspaper and school calendar that asked interested individuals to contact the school district. In addition, the school newsletter regularly features volunteer-related stories. But, says Housman, word of mouth has been the most effective marketing tool with the program's target audience—senior citizens.

"They talk among their friends about what they're doing and other things going on, and that's how the group has grown," she says.

To expand participation, Housman plans to use another popular outreach method—speaking to community clubs and service organizations. Regular appearances before these groups can lead to individual members volunteering or to the organization volunteering as a group. As Elizabeth Cayton, a principal in Windsor, North Carolina, discovered, soliciting a group for volunteers can lead to a chain reaction of similar requests.

"I talked to the minister's association about recruiting volunteers from church congregations. One minister belongs to the Kiwanis Club, and he asked fellow club members to volunteer. I now have people calling me to ask if they can volunteer, and they're hearing about our program from other folks," she says.

Additional means of reaching the nonparent audience include the following:

- *Bulletin boards*. Principals and/or program coordinators who want to boost participation from a specific group should find out where group members congregate and post notices there, says Mentoring Coordinator Linda Deafenbaugh, of Pittsburgh, Pennsylvania. She posted fliers on bulletin boards in the senior citizen center to increase the participation of senior citizens in school events. "Our recruitment fliers get more notice on bulletin boards because bulletin boards address issues of concern to seniors, [such as] Medicare and Social Security," she says.

- *Communitywide mailings*. Whenever a school mailing will reach the entire community, program and contact information should be included, and one or two specific volunteer jobs should be described. A past issue of Principal Charles Scott's school newsletter in Carmel, Indiana, called for volunteers to make voice recordings of library books for students who are auditory learners.

- *Church contacts*. Churches attract a good cross section of the population, which makes them an excellent place to reach a variety of groups. Neighborhood churches should be asked to feature a school volunteer program in their newsletters.

- *Fliers and pamphlets*. Written material featuring the program's goals, a description of volunteer opportunities, an invitation to participate, and contact information can be distributed locally through businesses. "We drop copies off at stores or post them on community bulletin boards at the mall," says Glenn Frank, principal in Moretown, Vermont.

Fliers and pamphlets can also be included with information sent to individuals who inquire about specific school programs or student registration or request other information.

- *Radio and television*. Even though they are expensive, public service announcements reach a large audience quickly and deliver the message repeatedly. Formal announcements most likely will be produced at the district level, but a related option at far less cost should not be overlooked: advertisements on public-access television.

- *Internet*. Schools with access to the Internet should consider adding a link that describes the volunteer program and lists specific volunteer opportunities.

Program Flexibility

Adding flexibility and variety to volunteer work assignments and to the program's general requirements can attract more nontraditional volunteers to the school. Publicizing non–student-related volunteer options, such as assembling bulletin boards, organizing special events, or helping to produce the school newsletter will appeal to individuals who may be interested in helping the school but are not interested in working directly with students. A range of opportunities that appeal to both genders can also improve recruitment.

Schools that help parents meet their own needs also are more likely to receive parent volunteer assistance. Volunteer Management Consultant Debbie Smith, who is a former coordinator of parents for the Reno, Nevada, school district, says it is wise to recognize and accommodate parents' busy schedules and child-care obligations when asking for help. "Many parents don't volunteer because they can't get [to the school] or because no one is available to take care of their [children]. We provide free transportation from central locations so parents who don't have cars can volunteer. We use volunteers to provide on-site child care as well," she says.

Eli Baker, principal in Sumter, South Carolina, gives individuals the option to volunteer to work from their homes, which has helped to generate interest and to retain volunteers. "If they didn't have the option of working at home, we'd lose them," he says. Volunteers' home assignments have included creating bulletin board decorations, designing maps and charts, and building playground equipment.

Parent Audience

Reaching the parent audience is far easier than reaching the community at large, because parents receive more frequent communications from the school and because they have a vested interest in the school—their children. Volunteer information can simply be made a standard feature of existing school-to-home communications and featured at school events. In fact, Michael Dietz, principal at Lake Shore Middle School in Mequon, Wisconsin, says that registration and back-to-school nights are excellent times to recruit volunteers. "It's hard for [people] to say no when you ask them personally," he says.

Additional ideas for reaching potential parent volunteers include the following:

- Solicit help from the Parent–Teacher Organization, which has a mailing list of all parents.
- Include volunteer information in the student–parent handbook.
- Send fliers or letters home with students.
- Add a "volunteer update" section to the school newsletter.
- Give parents volunteer information at school registration.
- Ask parents personally for help.

Screening Volunteers

All potential volunteers should be thoroughly screened, to guard student safety and to maintain program organization. Typical screening steps should include completion of an application form and a personal interview, as well as a criminal background check of the applicant.

Housman says that individuals interested in her program begin the application process by completing a volunteer application form, which is reviewed by the district's elementary school principals. "I run this by them to see if they know of any reason why the applicant should not be considered to be a volunteer," she says.

Most volunteer applications ask for standard information, including the applicant's name, address, telephone number, children's names (if any), availability, work preferences, and personal references. Some applications ask more detailed questions about specific skills the individual can offer the school. The sample Survey of Interest for Volunteers (Exhibit 4–1) includes a checklist on which applicants can quickly identify skills and interests. It is easy for potential volunteers to complete, and it is easy for staff to identify volunteer interests from the survey.

As part of the screening process, Housman reviews applications for completeness. Applicants must provide at least three references. Those who do not are not called for the next step in the process—a personal interview with the principal of the school where they would like to volunteer. Applicants who complete these first and second phases of screening are moved on to the final phase—a background check. As with prospective employees, volunteer background checks should be twofold: a check of references and a review of the individual's criminal background.

Reference checks may be conducted over the telephone or through the mail. Telephone checks are more immediate, but written checks allow references time to think about their answers and, perhaps, be more open. Exhibit 4–2 is a sample letter that may be sent to references identified on application forms. On it are seven

Exhibit 4–1   Survey of Interest for Volunteers (Sample)

You are invited! As a volunteer, you can help children learn.

Please share your time, skills, or interests with our students. You need not be experienced in teaching, just willing to share. The gift will help our students develop positive attitudes toward learning and motivate them to achieve their potential.

On the form below, please indicate how you are willing to help. We have provided a list to give you some ideas. We welcome your suggestions. This form may be returned in person or by mail to any school office. We will contact you regarding future involvement. Thank you!

Your name	Telephone (Area/No.) (Daytime) (Evening)

Address

Names and grades of your children, if any, attending our schools

I am willing to help students by

❏ coming to school   ❏ working from my home   ❏ no preference

I prefer to work at (name of school)

I prefer to work with the following students

❏ elementary   ❏ middle school   ❏ high school   ❏ no preference

I have the following skills to share:

❏ sewing/needlecraft
❏ working with one child
❏ typing/word processing
❏ working with a small group
❏ making phone calls
❏ making a presentation to a class
❏ cutting paper shapes
❏ installing/designing bulletin boards
❏ working with simple carpentry

❏ shelving/cataloguing books
❏ filing
❏ posting fliers in the neighborhood
❏ making posters/banners
❏ providing child care
❏ reading stories to children or listening to them read
❏ bookkeeping
❏ keeping score at athletic events
❏ working on publicity

❏ helping with math or science skills
❏ providing transportation
❏ organizing school events or fund-raisers
❏ chaperoning field trips, bus trips, or dances
❏ writing grants
❏ school decision making or advisory committees
❏ talking about career

Other ways I could help

My other hobbies/skills (e.g., camping, architecture, Swedish cooking, local history, calligraphy) are

I have access to

❏ typewriter or word processor   ❏ pickup truck or van   ❏ audiotape recorder   ❏ video camera

Source: Reprinted from *Survey of Interest for Volunteers (Appendix)*, with permission of the Wisconsin Department of Public Instruction, John T. Benson, Superintendent.

questions, four of which ask references to explain why they feel the applicant would or would not be a productive volunteer. One question asks references to rate the applicant in seven areas, including cooperativeness, patience, and confidence. The form can be mailed with a postage-paid envelope in which references can return the form to the school.

Questions to consider asking all references, whether contacted over the phone or via mail, include the following:

- How long have you known this person?
- How well do you know this person?
- How would you describe this person?
- Do you believe this person would be well suited for a volunteer position doing (fill in with specific activity)?
- Would this person be responsible and reliable?
- Has this person had similar volunteer experience in the past? If so, doing what?
- Is there anything about this person that makes you think he or she would not be appropriate for this volunteer position?

A criminal background review of potential volunteers should be conducted to identify individuals who may have a history of abuse but have been able to hide it. Although review regulations vary by state, the applicant typically must give the school permission to request criminal information from the state. Therefore, a permission clause on the application form or a separate, signed form giving permission for a background check is required before this step can be implemented. The necessary information should then be forwarded to the law enforcement agency providing the background check, as with prospective employees.

When the screening process is complete, most principals and program coordinators place applicants on a volunteer list and match them with staff members needing their skills. Because Housman's volunteer program is sanctioned by the school board, she presents the list of new volunteers to the school board for approval before assigning specific tasks.

Assigning Volunteers

One of the most valuable assets of a volunteer program, according to Housman, is a committed coordinator. "It's not easy for teachers to open their doors to outsiders. If teachers trust the person who's sending them the volunteers, though, they'll be more receptive to having another adult in their classrooms," she says. "Teachers also have to feel comfortable going to the coordinator if they believe [that] there's a compatibility problem and that the problem can be resolved fairly through the coordinator."

Friction between volunteers and teachers can be minimized by matching teacher needs and volunteer desires before the two parties join forces. Two documents, a volunteer job description and a staff request for a volunteer, are helpful in this process.

The volunteer job description defines the volunteer role at school and describes specific responsibilities, such as tasks, time commitment, attendance requirements, extent of authority, and communication channels.

The Teacher Request for Volunteer Service (Exhibit 4–3) also specifies what the volunteer will do and when he or she is needed. This information enables the principal or coordinator to match volunteers and teachers according to staff needs and volunteer interests, which are identified on the volunteer application form. Staff members requesting volunteer assistance should submit both documents to the principal or coordinator simultaneously to ensure an optimum match.

When placing volunteers, administrators will sometimes be faced with a parent who insists on working in his or her child's

Exhibit 4–2   Volunteer Screening Reference Letter (Sample)

Dear _____ :   _____ (Date)

_____ has applied for a volunteer position

with the _____ (School/Program). Your name has been given as a personal reference. Please complete this form and return it in the enclosed envelope.

The program provides meaningful volunteer activities. Volunteers respond to local community needs in many human service areas throughout the area.

Volunteer position applied for: _____

1. How long have you know the applicant? _____

2. How well do you know the applicant? (Check)
   ❑ very well   ❑ well   ❑ average   ❑ little   ❑ very little

3. Your relationship to the applicant: (Check)   ❑ co-worker ❑ employer ❑ friend
   ❑ relative   ❑ other (Please specify) _____

4. In your opinion, would this person be a responsible and reliable volunteer for the position applied for?
   ❑ Yes   ❑ No (Please explain)

5. Would you recommend the applicant as a volunteer with our program?
   ❑ Yes   ❑ No (Please explain)

6. Is there anything about this individual that would cause difficulty in participation as a volunteer? (If so, what?)

7. Please check the column that best describes the applicant.

	Usually	**Sometimes**	**Never**	**Don't Know**
Cooperative	❑	❑	❑	❑
Calm under stress	❑	❑	❑	❑
Patient	❑	❑	❑	❑
Well adjusted	❑	❑	❑	❑
Confident	❑	❑	❑	❑
Personable	❑	❑	❑	❑
Able to make decisions	❑	❑	❑	❑

Reference's Signature	Date signed
➤	

Thank you for completing this form. Please return it to (Name of school volunteer coordinator and school's address)

_____

_____

Courtesy of RSVP of Dane County, Madison, Wisconsin.

Exhibit 4–3   Teacher Request for Volunteer Service

Teacher's Name	Grade	Date of request
Position	Days volunteer(s) needed	
Time of day volunteer(s) needed	Amount of time needed	

Activities for Volunteers

Academic

- ❑ Listen to students read.
- ❑ Conduct flash card drills.
- ❑ Tell stories to students.
- ❑ Help students use IMC resources.
- ❑ Tape-record texbooks so that students who have reading problems can listen to cassettes as they read their assignments.
- ❑ Assist in science and math labs.
- ❑ Help in vocational classrooms and labs, such as agribusiness, business/marketing, and technology education classes.
- ❑ Hep students who have been absent make up missed work.
- ❑ Assist non–English-speaking students in expanding their vocabulary/conversation.
- ❑ Play instructional games.
- ❑ Other: Please use this area to further clarify your request or to explain a need not on the checklist.

Exceptional Needs

- ❑ Work with underachievers.
- ❑ Prepare tactile material for visually impaired students.
- ❑ Assist special education teacher in giving students extra drill and reinforcing concepts.
- ❑ Help students share their own experiences, such as what it is like to be a person with a disability and how the disability impacts on relationships and career choices.
- ❑ Work on perceptual activities.
- ❑ Work with children with disabilities.
- ❑ Help students with motor skill problems.
- ❑ Reinforce specific skills.
- ❑ Talk to children; be a friend.
- ❑ Help with handwriting practice.

Enrichment

- ❑ Prepare bulletin boards.
- ❑ Make props for plays.
- ❑ Gather resource materials.
- ❑ Help students with keyboarding.
- ❑ Help students with arts and crafts.
- ❑ Make lists of resource materials.
- ❑ Discuss careers, training opportunities, and college selection.
- ❑ Bring in community resource people to speak on experiences and expertise.
- ❑ Describe personal participation in political campaigns and local history.
- ❑ Encourage and assist in fine arts.
- ❑ Help students with foreign language.
- ❑ Play musical instruments for students.
- ❑ Dramatize a story.
- ❑ Discuss/participate in special occasions/holidays.
- ❑ Demonstrate hobbies, pioneer crafts, and special interests.
- ❑ Provide time to illustrate, organize, and print writing projects.
- ❑ Assist staffs of student publications, yearbooks, newspapers, and audiovisual productions.
- ❑ Show personal slides.

I understand that this request is not a guarantee of receiving volunteer help, as the availability of volunteers varies.

Name of school

Teacher's Signature   Date

➤

Principal's Signature   Date

➤

Courtesy of the Janesville School District, Janesville, Wisconsin.

classroom—a situation that raises an important question. Should a parent volunteer be placed in his or her child's classroom, or should the parent and the child always be separated?

Principals and volunteer coordinators disagree on what effect the practice has on the student, his or her performance, and the classroom teacher. "I've done it both ways, and I really don't find one method better than the other," says Principal Karol Sonnamaker. "There are pros and cons to each one."

Supporters of the arrangement maintain that student behavior actually improves when parents are in the room. Because they want parent approval, students work harder to do well, to act appropriately, and to help when needed. Those who oppose placing parents and children in the same room say that the parent's presence puts additional pressure on teachers, because they know the parent will look out for his or her child. "I had a teacher who didn't know how to effectively discipline an aide's child because she thought the volunteer was second-guessing her methods," says Baker.

Staff Training and Resistance

Because education is a "people profession," administrators often assume that faculty and staff know how to work with volunteers when, in fact, they may not. Programs can benefit from regular reminders to staff about using volunteer resources.

Principal Glenn Frank each year reviews basic volunteer-related information, including channels of communication with teachers. Principal Barb Patrick, because she can devote only limited time to training, invites a volunteer coordinator from a neighboring district to brief staff on appropriate volunteer tasks and planning. The coordinator asks teachers to keep lists of the ways in which volunteers could help them. This reinforces to staff members that "they can't just wait until the volunteer shows up and then try to find something for him or her to do," she says.

Secretaries should be reminded of their importance to volunteer programs, too, says volunteer Management Consultant Smith. Most volunteers' first impressions of a school are based on the office staff, so a welcoming attitude is imperative. "If the secretary flashes an upbeat, glad-you're-here smile and speaks in a pleasant tone, volunteers will feel comfortable in school. If the secretary treats volunteers as a nuisance or an inconvenience, they probably won't come back," she says.

Although most teachers welcome volunteers, some resist having another adult in the classroom. Principals and supervisors of volunteers address these situations on a case-by-case basis, but they report the greatest amount of success with a "soft sell" approach. Patricia Chamberlain, principal in Sharon, Connecticut, pairs hesitant teachers with an especially cooperative volunteer to work on a specific, short-term task, often not classroom based, such as making books. "The teacher can experience quick success and therefore will be more likely to continue using volunteer help," she says.

Teachers at Dena Wheeler's Afton, Iowa, school are gently reminded of the clear limits placed on volunteer authority. "Our volunteer orientation manual clearly states that the teacher runs the classroom," she says. "It also explains how volunteers need to follow teachers' directions at all times."

Wheeler, a volunteer coordinator and teacher, adds that this strategy builds teachers' sense of security because they know they won't be "upstaged by a volunteer."

Other administrators encourage teachers to visit colleague's classrooms where they can see volunteer contributions firsthand. They can see that volunteers are background players, not obtrusive know-it-alls who challenge teacher expertise and authority.

Sometimes no action is the best action when staff members resist working with volunteers, says Karol Sonnamaker, principal in Eunice, New Mexico. Discussions with colleagues who talk about how volunteers help them and the passage of time soften resistors' perception of volunteers. "Sometimes a teacher will say, 'Look what this parent did,' and show off a new bulletin board. It doesn't take long for the nonbelievers to change their minds," she says.

Training Volunteers

New volunteers, like new employees, require an orientation to the school to act appropriately and to be effective in their roles. "By and large, we've avoided problems with volunteers because our orientation trains them before they ever go into the classroom," says Patrick. "[Volunteers] understand their role, which eliminates a lot of problems right away."

Issues

The principal and/or volunteer coordinator who screens and places volunteers should review with them basic nuts-and-bolts information about the school building, general staff policies, and specific volunteer obligations.

Building layout, rules, and policies. Volunteers should be provided with general information, such as the location of staff restrooms, parking, and personal storage areas, as well as supply requisition procedures, to acclimate them to the school atmosphere and expectations. Because volunteers are subject to many of the same policies as regular staff, a formal review of those policies allows administrators and/or coordinators to clarify expectations and to answer policy-related questions.

Program expectations. After volunteers are familiar with the school itself, general expectations should be discussed. These include signing in and out, logging hours, and notifying the school if they cannot attend when scheduled. "You must give them very clear-cut guidelines about the commitment they're making," says Housman.

Also explain that problems should be brought to the attention of the administrator and/or coordinator on the first occurrence, to avoid serious, ongoing conflicts. "Make it very clear during orientation that if parent volunteers don't feel comfortable in a classroom or believe there may be a potential conflict, they should be open and aboveboard about it," says Sonnamaker.

Most volunteer problems are little more than personality conflicts, says Chet Hubbard, principal in Lubec, Maine, and can be resolved if addressed early. "Leaving it alone only makes it worse," he says. "But if there are no hard feelings between the two [parties], I can usually reassign the volunteer or redefine his or her responsibilities. Unfortunately, I've had instances where it was January before a problem came to my attention. By that time, most issues are emotionally charged, and they're more difficult to resolve."

Interaction and physical contact. One of the most volatile issues confronting volunteer programs is the threat of abuse charges against volunteers and the school. Volunteers must be well versed in how to interact with children and how, when, and to what extent they can touch students, says Housman. "We stress that volunteers can't be too affectionate with the children, which some seniors have a difficult time understanding."

Sonnamaker tells volunteers the same thing she tells her teaching staff—they can touch students, but with caution and common sense. "I stress that they need to be careful how and where they touch students and that they should never touch a student in anger. Even if no physical harm takes place, it could give the appearance that the volunteer is assaulting a student," she says.

Paul A. Millichap, an attorney with the Chicago law firm of Franczek, Sullivan, Mann, Crement, Hein, and Relias, PC, says the "generally accepted" rule is that volunteers can touch a child if the purpose is for direction or restraint. Students who are fighting, for example, can be held so they don't harm themselves or others. "Touching for comfort, however, is no longer permitted or encouraged by most schools," he says.

During training sessions, Millichap recommends that principals and/or volunteer coordinators role-play which types of touching are acceptable and which are not. "Talking about touching is one thing, but when volunteers see it acted out, it's far more effective," he says.

Millichap adds that volunteers should also avoid situations in which they are alone with students and that doors to their work areas should always remain open.

General liability issues. The proper role of volunteers, according to Millichap, is to "assist, not take the place of, certified staff. The important thing to remember is that schools should never put volunteers in a position where they're substitutes for teachers."

To prevent situations in which volunteers assume more responsibility than is legal, explain to them the differences between their role and the role of teachers and school staff. For example, volunteers can correct student assignments and examinations if they are responsible only for determining if answers are correct. Under no circumstances should volun-

teers be asked to fulfill a teacher's responsibility, as would be the case if the volunteer were making an educational judgment about how well a student had mastered a skill. "Teachers can ask volunteers to assist them but not to take over basic responsibilities like grading homework or supervising the class," says Frank.

Nor should volunteers be made responsible for students' physical well-being. Principal Ken Graham of Parsippany, New Jersey, says that if a parent volunteer is supervising a group of 5–10 students, "there will always be a teacher involved. Volunteers can share an experience like this, but we don't put them in a position of responsibility for it."

Confidentiality. By their very presence in school, volunteers will learn highly personal information about students, including health conditions, behavioral problems, family arrangements, grades, and special needs. They must understand that specific, school-related information cannot be discussed with family or friends. Some program supervisors even advise volunteers to treat school-related information as they would a physician–patient or attorney–client relationship.

Suspected child abuse is a specific confidentiality-related situation that should be reviewed with all volunteers. According to Millichap, volunteers should not necessarily go straight to the authorities with their suspicions. Instead, they should be made aware of what child abuse is and given information about whom they should take their concerns to, he says.

Regarding information that may be discussed publicly, Patrick distinguishes between that which volunteers can divulge and that which is best left to teachers. "Volunteers can talk about positive things that go on at school. But if something really wonderful happens to a student, [such as] winning a prestigious award, I want the teacher, not volunteers, to tell parents," she says.

Evaluation. If applicable, volunteers should be told when, how, and on what criteria they will be evaluated. This is best done during training given by specific classroom teachers and/or appropriate staff members when volunteers begin working directly with students or projects. This policy helps volunteers to recognize the limits of their roles and to understand staff member expectations and the goals of classroom activities.

As an example, Housman cites curriculum. "It's very important that the training include a broad presentation of the curriculum covered in a particular school system, grade, or building," she says. "Volunteers need to have some idea of the math concepts covered and whole language, for instance."

Handbooks for Volunteers

Much of the information conveyed during orientation sessions can be summarized in a volunteer handbook. This publication can serve as a standing reference for volunteers, and it also can act as a summary of the overall program that may be distributed to individuals considering becoming volunteers.

The following information should be considered for inclusion in a volunteer handbook:

- welcome letter
- basic school information (e.g., staff roster, school calendar, school hours, phone numbers, building map, and information on the supervisor who volunteers should contact with concerns)
- basic school policies and procedures (e.g., dress code, telephone calls, smoking, chain of command, dismissal procedures, disaster drills, personal belongings, and injuries)
- general curriculum overview and school discipline philosophy
- volunteer job description
- responsibilities of volunteers and rules of conduct (e.g., being on time, notification in the case of absence, sign in on arrival)
- application and screening procedures
- statement on confidentiality and code of ethics
- tips on working with students
- tips on working with staff
- evaluation procedure
- process for handling problems and conflicts with staff

Letter to Parents

Principal William Heasley, of Tarentum, Pennsylvania, alerts parents with a letter whenever a student will be working one-on-one with a volunteer.

"This adds a measure of confidentiality because parents become more sensitive to what school volunteers are saying. If they hear something about their child, they can bring that information to us, and we can stop the leak."

Dietz agrees that notifying parents that their son or daughter will be working with a volunteer is a wise practice. "It gives parents a chance to talk about why the student needs to do this in the first place, and it gives them an opportunity to object. You don't have to explain after the fact why you're doing what you're doing," he says.

Communication with Volunteers

How volunteer problems are dealt with directly affects a school's volunteer retention rate. Unresolved conflicts and/or confusion about roles and responsibilities will prompt volunteers to take their time and abilities elsewhere, which is likely to damage the school's word-of-mouth community relations as well.

Constant communication with volunteers and their supervising teachers and/or staff members, along with the flexibility to adjust assignments, can lessen problems caused by volunteer mismatches, says Housman. It also can help keep volunteers interested and willing to participate in school activities. To ensure that volunteers feel comfortable in their positions, she talks with each volunteer at least once every 2 or 3 months. If problems exist, she intervenes before they escalate.

"One volunteer was a former math teacher who was assigned to a sixth grade classroom. [The assignment] was an abysmal failure," says Housman. "He said he wanted to take over the class for 40 minutes once a week and teach a math concept in game form. I reassigned him to teachers who were interested in this, and everyone, including the volunteer, is thrilled."

In another situation, Housman kept a veteran volunteer from quitting after learning that the volunteer's relationship with a new teacher started tenuously. "The teacher didn't contact the volunteer quickly [after learning of the assignment], which upset the volunteer," she says. "I talked with the teacher, who immediately called the volunteer. The teacher had not realized the volunteer was so desirous of hearing from her right away. Now things are great between them."

Ongoing communication with volunteers also results in more enthusiastic participation, says Principal Betty Replogle, of Beatrice, Nebraska. "Too often schools believe they know what works best, so they shut out suggestions from volunteers. I think we have to be open to those ideas if we want volunteers to truly cooperate with us," she says.

Principal Scott meets weekly with the president of the Parent–Teacher Organi-

zation to discuss serious or controversial issues. The president, in turn, communicates school news to members. "It has made a difference [in members' attitudes] because they know I'm not trying to hide anything from them. Volunteers are now some of my strongest allies," he says.

Evaluation of Volunteers and Program

Annual evaluations of individual volunteers and of the volunteer program itself will help improve the overall quality of the program. Parent Coordinator Debbie Smith uses a three-step assessment tool to pinpoint areas for improvement. The first step is a volunteer self-evaluation; the second step is a teacher evaluation of the volunteer; and the third step is a volunteer evaluation of the program. All but the self-evaluation are completed at the end of the school year, she says. These evaluations occur early in the volunteer experience.

"This way volunteers can take a serious look at what they're doing and whether or not they enjoy it. If they're not happy, they can be reassigned," says Smith.

Exhibits 4–4 and 4–5 are sample evaluation forms that may be used as models while principals/coordinators develop their own tools for evaluation of the program. Exhibit 4–4 is a form for the volunteer's evaluation of the long-term program—if the volunteer works with school staff for an entire year, for example. Exhibit 4–5 is a form for use by a short-term volunteer and for individuals who volunteer on a single-assignment basis.

CONCLUSION

Managing a successful volunteer program is, in many ways, not much different from managing a regular staff. It re-

Exhibit 4–4   School Volunteer's Evaluation of Program (Sample)

Volunteer's Name	School

Teacher's/Supervisor's Name

1. Describe what you do as a school volunteer:

2. How would you describe your volunteer experience?
   ❏ Excellent   ❏ Good   ❏ Satisfactory   ❏ Unsatisfactory

3. Does the teacher ask you how the students are doing?   ❏ Yes   ❏ No

4. Does the teacher let you know how you are doing?   ❏ Yes   ❏ No
   In what way?

5. Do you think you have adequate time to discuss the students and assignments with the teacher?   ❏ Yes   ❏ No   *Comments*:

6. Are you regular in attendance?   ❏ Always   ❏ Most of the time   ❏ Sometimes
   If there are problems, please describe:

7. How would you rate the relationship you have with the students?
   ❏ Excellent   ❏ Good   ❏ Satisfactory   ❏ Unsatisfactory

8. Do you work with any of the following minorities? If so, *how many* have you helped during the year?
   ____ African American   ____ American Indian   ____ Asian/Pacific Islander
   ____ Biracial   ____ Spanish/Hispanic   ____ Handicapped

9. How do the teacher(s)/supervisor and student(s) show you that you are appreciated?

10. Would you like to work with the same teacher/supervisor next year?
    ❏ Yes   ❏ No   *If no, please explain*:

11. How could the staff be more helpful to you?

12. May this information be shared with your teacher/supervisor?   ❏ Yes   ❏ No

13. Other comments:

Courtesy of RSVP of Dane County, Madison, Wisconsin.

Exhibit 4–5   Volunteer's Evaluation of Short-Term School Program (Sample)

Return to school volunteer coordinator

Date of Assignment	Date Request Received
School	Teacher's or Supervisor's Name
Volunteer's Name	
Volunteer's Assignment	Total Hours per Assignment

What were the strengths of the assignment?

What were the weaknesses of the assignment?

Would you accept this type of program again? ❑ Yes ❑ No	How did the children react to the program? ❑ Excellent ❑ Good ❑ Fair ❑ Poor	Did the children appear to be comfortable with you? ❑ Yes ❑ No

Other comments:

Courtesy of RSVP of Dane County, Madison, Wisconsin.

quires careful screening and placement of individuals who participate, providing regular feedback to volunteers, and giving annual evaluations. Careful management in all areas and appropriate attention to liability issues can substantially bolster the degree of type 3 involvement in schools. This management strategy is successful because potential volunteers know that the program has structure and direction and that they won't be arbitrarily placed and left to fend for themselves.

CHAPTER 5

Type 4 Involvement: At-Home Learning and Coaching

To promote type 4 involvement, school leaders should provide information and ideas to families about how to help students at home with homework and other curriculum-related decisions and planning.

Schools are most effective when parents reinforce messages students receive from teachers, says Stephen Kleinsmith, assistant superintendent in Millard, Nebraska. "If we want children to have high expectations of learning, then parents must regularly send those sorts of signals. They need to be involved. They need to show children that learning is a lifelong activity, and that they're working with the school as a team. Students at all levels tend toward higher levels of commitment to their schooling when their parents are involved. Children get better grades and score higher on national standardized tests, and the number of behavior and discipline problems [goes] down when parents are involved," he says.

RESEARCH FINDINGS

For more than 10 years, researchers have shown that parent involvement in school activities improves student attitudes and performance, enhances students' self-esteem, improves academic achievement, builds positive parent–child relationships, and helps parents to develop positive attitudes toward school and the educational process. A search of digest information compiled by US Department of Education's Educational Resources Information Center shows that many published reports support these assertions.

Parent involvement can offset negative external influences on children, such as poverty. Chavkin and Gonzalez[1] write that one of the most promising ways to increase students' achievement is to involve their families.[2,3] Walberg[4] found that family participation in education was twice as predictive of academic learning as family socioeconomic status. Establishing partnerships with families has many benefits for schools and families, but Epstein[5(p.701)] says, "the main reason to create such partnerships is to help all youngsters succeed in school and in later life."

Involvement in school activities may improve parent self-image. Becher[6] summarizes research by Herman and Yeh,[7] indicating "that parents involved in child care and educational programs develop positive attitudes about themselves, increase self-confidence, and often enroll in programs to enhance their personal development. They also are more positive about school and school personnel than uninvolved parents."

Student achievement and attitudes, inside and outside school, improve with parent involvement. Both Becher and Peterson[8] state that students' overall attitudes toward school and participation rates improve when parents actively participate in activities. Becher writes, "Substantial evidence exists to show that children whose parents are involved in their schooling have significantly increased their academic achievement and cognitive development."[9] Peterson[10] says, "Children whose parents are involved in their formal education have many advantages. They have better grades, test scores, long-term academic achievement, attitudes, and behavior than those with disinterested mothers and fathers."[11]

Researchers at the Search Institute in Minneapolis, Minnesota, have also analyzed parent involvement and found that students in grades 6–12 with involved parents tend to be more motivated in school and more committed to continuing education beyond high school. The institute, which analyzed surveys of 170,000 public school students in 250 school districts, also found that "problem behaviors such as alcohol use, violence and antisocial behavior decrease as parent involvement increases."[12]

STRATEGIES

At-Home Learning and Coaching

One of the most efficient ways to involve parents and improve student performance is to recruit the help of parents in the home. At-home learning and coaching extends learning beyond the classroom and can maintain or improve overall levels of parent involvement at the middle and upper grade levels, where it typically drops.

According to Kleinsmith, involvement peaks at the early grade levels, then falls off rapidly as children mature. "It's common to see a drastic drop-off in parental involvement from the sixth through the twelfth grades. At the elementary level, children like having their parents stop in for lunch or for cookies and milk. But teenagers usually don't feel that it's 'cool'

to have their parents in school with them anymore, so parents stop coming," he says.

Statistics show that parents of adolescents are interested in their children's education and that many do, indeed, talk about school with their children in the home. *Youth Indicators 1993* reports that 85–91 percent of eighth-grade students talk with their parents about school-related issues and 90 percent of parents check students' homework.[13] The report also indicates, however, that parent involvement drops off significantly as participation requirements are added. This is especially true when involvement requires direct contact between parent and school. Sixty percent of students surveyed reported that their parents had spoken with a teacher or counselor at their school; only 29 percent said that a parent had actually visited a school classroom.

Kleinsmith advocates rethinking the basic structure of parent involvement programs to counteract this trend. "Schools know that as children mature, their needs change. What schools don't realize is that parents' needs are changing, as well, but their opportunities to be involved at the school usually stay the same. As children change chronologically and emotionally, so should the way parents are involved in school," he says.

At-home parent help actually is the preferred method of parent involvement among older students. Kleinsmith says, "We looked at one study in particular that asked 1,300 students, 'What's the best way to have your parents involved in school?' The students' reply was that they liked it when parents could help them with homework—to check [whether] they'd solved their math problems correctly and give assistance when needed."

The result of this research was the formation and implementation of a series of parenting classes designed to help parents be better able to help their children with homework (Resource 5–1). "The sessions teach parents the same concepts their children are learning, as well as teaching techniques they can use when students ask for help," Kleinsmith says. Joanie Wilson, the teacher who sponsors and conducts the sessions, says they have also improved home-to-school communication, a type 2 form of involvement.

The Education Technology Training Center at the Bridgeport Public Schools in Bridgeport, Connecticut, is also giving parents basic computer skills that they can use to help students when assignments require use of computer technology, according to Raymond Krish, education technology coordinator. Many parents there do not own home computers and are not computer literate. The center offers beginning, intermediate, and advanced courses free of charge, for parents to learn about computer technology and how their children use it at school. Resource 5–2 explains how the Education Technology Training Center, which won a 1996 Magna Award for excellence in education, helps parents come up to speed with computer technology so they can help their children with computer projects. Community donations and volunteers played key roles in the center's beginning, and it continues to generate widespread community support.

Ascher[14] notes Walberg's suggestion[15] that when parents have limited time, as is typical with single and working parents, one of the most efficient activities for parents is helping their children with home-based learning projects. At-home learning is also both a natural and a convenient extension of school, according to Rich.[16] Since students spend far more time with parents than with teachers, parents are presented with far more "teachable moments" that can be used to reinforce concepts learned in school.[17]

Epstein[18] has also proved the value of home-based learning. Her work suggests that one effective strategy is to send work packets home for students and parents to complete together. Seventh-grade students who were given an English achievement test at the beginning of the school year earned scores similar to those earned at the end of their sixth-grade year. But for students who had marginal skills, the summer study packets given to the test group were related to increased test scores.

Mercedes Fitzmaurice of Research for Better Schools, in Philadelphia, Pennsylvania, recommends at-home activities as well, but adds that they do not have to be strictly principle- or content-related. One of the activities her organization suggests is to give students an assignment to interview their parents or family members. Examples of questions are as follows: What was your most frightening moment? When and how did you learn to do your favorite activity? What is your earliest memory? Students can then share answers in small groups or write them in story form as part of a booklet, with pictures, about their family. This type of activity brings schools and families together in nontraditional ways and helps students to exercise a variety of skills—brainstorming questions, speaking, note taking, organizing, and writing.

Brown[19] writes that "some activities can be adapted to almost any home situation. These are activities that parents or children engage in on a day-to-day basis." She suggests activities such as preparing questions about television programs that students watch with their parents and including children in meal preparation and grocery shopping.

A slightly different strategy for involving parents in home learning is used in Monroe, North Carolina, where parents can earn the rank of "five-star parent" by living up to obligations outlined in the Five-Star Parent Program. The program, which began in 1994, is cosponsored by the city Chamber of Commerce and won a 1996 Magna Award for excellence.

According to a description supplied by the district's public information officer, Luan C. Ingram, parents who participate in the program sign a special report card, which serves as a contract requiring them to participate in their children's education in four areas: expecting academic achievement and progress, participating in school activities, performing at-home follow-up, and promoting social and emotional development. Among the activities specified are establishing a reward system for students when they do well in school, attending a Parent–Teacher Association or Parent–Teacher Organization meeting or open house, reading or reviewing homework with students at least twice a week, and attending a parenting workshop.

Parents who meet all requirements are recognized by the principal of the school their children attend. They also receive a vehicle window sticker that says, "Proud Kid of a Five-Star Parent." After the program's first year, 26 percent of all elementary and middle school parents became five-star parents. Thirty-three percent of all elementary school parents participated.

Communicating Parent Responsibility

To cultivate partnerships with parents, it is often necessary to remind them that they have an important at-home role to play in student learning. Kleinsmith recommends that faculty and staff initially stress the topic with parents by sharing the following list of involvement responsibilities and options:

- Call or visit the school staff on a regular basis, and talk with teachers before problems occur. Don't wait until trouble occurs to make the first contact.
- Attend special events at your child's school, such as open house, parent–teacher conferences, curriculum night, booster club meetings, and Parent–Teacher Association or Parent–Teacher Organization meetings. Also make time to be involved in your child's cocurricular activities such as drama, music, and sports.
- Serve on school building and district advisory councils or committees.
- Volunteer your time as a tutor, classroom or recess aide, or secretarial aide or as a carpenter/repairman. Serve as a monitor during cocurricular activities such as dances, athletic events, and field trips, or serve as a judge for activities such as science fairs and art shows.
- Help proofread and edit the school newsletter.
- Give a guest lecture on career occupations and/or travel abroad.
- Become involved in the student's curriculum planning, and discuss academic options with your son or daughter.
- Encourage involvement in school activities of the student's choice.
- Ask your son or daughter, "What good questions did you ask today?" or "What did you learn in school today?" Then practice good listening, a key to effective communication.
- Encourage reading, using the library, and purchasing books at a young age.

CONCLUSION

Learning is a 24-hour activity, and research shows that schools should make greater efforts to educate families on this issue. Clearly, there are learning benefits from actively involving students in even such routine daily activities as grocery shopping or meal preparation. Resources 5–1 and 5–2 demonstrate some of the many opportunities that can help parents to understand how important home learning is and to improve their own skills, so they can be more helpful when the student needs them. Administrators are wise to evaluate the ways in which their school can provide these types of opportunities and to suggest that faculty develop take-home activities requiring parent and/or family involvement.

REFERENCES

1. N.F. Chavkin and D.L. Gonzalez, Forging Partnerships between Mexican–American Parents and Schools, *Educational Resources Information Center Digest*, ED388489 (Charleston, WV: ERIC Clearinghouse on Rural Education and Small Schools, 1995).

2. N.F. Chavkin, ed., *Families and Schools in a Pluralistic Society* (Albany, NY: State University of New York Press, 1993).

3. A.T. Henderson and N. Berla, eds., *A New Generation of Evidence: The Family Is Critical to Student Achievement* (Washington, DC: National Committee for Citizens in Education, 1994).

4. H.J. Walberg, Improving the Productivity of America's Schools, *Educational Leadership* 41, no. 8 (1984): 19–27.

5. J. Epstein, School/Family/Community Partnerships: Caring for the Children We Share, *Phi Delta Kappan* 76, no. 9 (1995): 701–712.

6. R. Becher, Parents and Schools, *Educational Resource Information Center Digest*, ED269137 (Urbana, IL: ERIC Clearinghouse on Elementary and Early Childhood Education, 1986).

7. J.L. Herman and J.P. Yeh, Some Effects of Parent Involvement in Schools, 1980.

8. D. Peterson, Parent Involvement in the Educational Process, *Educational Resource Information Center* Digest, ED312776 (Eugene, OR: ERIC Clearinghouse on Educational Management, 1989).

9. Becher, Parents and Schools.

10. Peterson, Parent Involvement in the Edcucational Process.

11. Peterson, Parent Involvement in the Educational Process.

12. "Connecting Schools and Families," *Search Institute Source* 10, no. 3 (1994): 1.

13. *Youth Indicators 1993*. Trends in the Well-Being of American Youth. National Center for Education Statistics, Office of Educational Research and Improvement, Washington, DC.

14. C. Ascher, Improving the School–Home Connection for Low-Income Urban Parents, *Educational Resources Information Center Digest*, ED293973 (New York: ERIC Clearinghouse on Urban Education, 1988).

15. H.J. Walberg, Families as Partners in Educational Productivity, *Phi Delta Kappan* 65, no. 6 (1983): 397–400.

16. D. Rich, *The Forgotten Factor in School Success: The Family. A Policymaker's Guide* (Washington, DC: The Home and School Institute, 1985).

17. Peterson, Parent Involvement in the Educational Process.

18. J.L. Epstein and S.C. Herrick, Implementation and Effects of Summer Home Learning Packets in the Middle Grades. Two Reports, *Educational Resource Information Center Digest*, ED339544 (Baltimore, MD: Center for Research on Effective School for Disadvantaged Students, 1991).

19. P.C. Brown, Involving Parents in the Education of their Children, *Educational Resources Information Center Digest*, ED308988 (Urbana, IL: ERIC Clearinghouse on Elementary and Early Childhood Education, 1989).

Resource 5–1

Parent Study Skill Review Nights

Millard Public Schools
Omaha, Nebraska

Issue addressed: Equipping parents with skills to help middle school students with mathematics assignments
Agencies involved: School, parents
Type of community: Suburban
Approximate student enrollment: 18,500
Start date: 1993

Program Description

Joanie Wilson, who teaches in the Millard Public Schools in Omaha, Nebraska, helps parents become more involved in their middle and high school students' activities by conducting Parent Study Skill Review Nights, a 4-week program that teaches parents basic mathematics concepts so they can provide help if students ask for it.

Wilson says that the sessions have helped parents to polish rusty mathematics skills and have opened parent communication with the school. "I had one parent call me about a scheduling problem that was completely beyond my control, but she called because she felt that we had established a relationship through review night. Without this, she probably wouldn't have asked the question at all," she says.

Structure and Goals

Because parents meet only once a week for 2 hours, the information presented isn't exhaustive. But sessions provide enough background that parents can think through problems with their students, says Wilson.

Each session focuses on a different topic, including geometry, algebra, calculators, and word problems. Wilson uses hands-on activities to give parents information and to teach problem-solving strategies. The geometry session, for example, features paper cutouts and folding activities to review terms. On that evening Wilson also talks about the development of visual and spatial ability and how geometry is especially difficult for students at the middle grades. During the algebra session, Wilson reviews the "BS Principle." "That simply means that you can do anything you want to the equation, but to solve it you have to do the same things to both sides," she says.

In addition to teaching review nights, Wilson writes mathematics-related articles for the school newsletter. Topics have included how parents can help their students study, how parents can help students ask good questions, and the myth of the "math gene." "I don't want parents giving their students an excuse to do poorly by saying they 'were never good at math' themselves," she says. "The reinforcement provided in these articles is one thing that parents have said they enjoy and find helpful."

Positive feedback and growing interest indicate that the program works. Class size more than doubled from the first year to the second. "I've received comments like, 'I've never understood the concept of the area of a circle' and 'I remember a lot more about math than I thought I did,'" says Wilson.

Parent Study Skill Review Nights are publicized through the school newsletters, at a study skills night for incoming sixth grade parents, and at open house.

Wilson says that both students and parents benefit from parents' participation in the review nights. Students, of course, have an additional resource when stumped by mathematics problems, and parents reach new comfort levels with the school. "After they spend four weeks with me, they feel good about the school, and they have a better understanding of the curriculum," says Wilson.

For more information about Parent Study Skill Review Nights, contact Millard Public Schools, 5606 South 147th Street, Omaha, NE 68137; telephone (402) 895-8200.

Resource 5–2

Education Technology Training Center

Bridgeport Public Schools
Bridgeport, Connecticut

Issue addressed: Empowering parents and helping them to understand the basics of computers and word processing, how the students are using computers in school, and strategies that can be used at home to help their children academically
Agencies involved: School district, parents, local university
Type of community: Urban
Approximate student enrollment: 20,000
Start date: 1995

Program Description and Goals

When parents are not familiar with computers and technology, it can be difficult for them to feel comfortable helping their children with assignments that incorporate computers. Superintendent James Connelly and the school board for Bridgeport Public Schools in Bridgeport, Connecticut, established a state-of-the-art computer training center for parents—the Education Technology Training Center.

Raymond Krish, the district's education technology coordinator, says the facility creates a place for parents to go and learn about what the students are learning on computers in school. "The local university donated an entire floor to house the ed tech center, while two computer corporations donated the software needed to supplement our network," says Krish. "The technology budget for the year, approximately $70,000, was dedicated toward the purchase of 23 computers, the file

servers, and additional software and furniture for the center."

The goal of the program is to educate parents to become computer literate so they can learn with the students. Because many families do not own a home computer, this computer laboratory allows parents to attend minicourses on the basics of computers, word processors, and office programs that produce spreadsheets.

"After just 18 months of operation, 7,000 to 8,000 parents have completed courses," says Krish. "Many of the parents who attend these classes return to the center to be an instructor or volunteer to help in the classrooms."

Courses

Schedules are spread out during the day to make it convenient for most parents to attend the course. Some classes are offered during school hours, while many are conducted at night. "Because of the overwhelming response to the program, we've added a couple of Saturday courses to our curriculum. The courses are free to parents and typically last from 2–10 hours," says Krish.

A typical computer course at the center is a basic 2-hour class that introduces parents to how personal computers can be used and provides an orientation to the functions a computer allows a person to do. A more advanced class might be courses dedicated to learning word processing, databases, and spreadsheets. "One popular course has been an elementary course that allows the [students] and parents to work side-by-side on a computer," says Krish.

The courses are led by teachers, parents who have completed the courses previously, and representatives from the business community. Krish explains that teachers who participate in weekend and evening classes receive a stipend, but all other instructors volunteer their time.

"When there are computers available in the tech center, parents are welcome to come in and practice their computer skills." However, sometimes when no courses are scheduled, the school plans for teacher training courses or after-school workshops.

Course listings are publicized in the superintendent's newsletter, the local newspaper, and regularly attended parent meetings. "The response has been outstanding, and the parents who have taken all the courses are enthused about volunteering [in] the classroom and aiding teachers on computer assignments," Krish says.

Keys to Success

Krish says the strength of the program lies in community support. "We were able to make this idea work [because of] the donations and volunteers from the community," he says. "When the ed tech center was started, we publicized it widely and introduced parents and community members to it.

"We sent home fliers with students to excite parents and urge them to participate in our programs to learn how technology is being integrated into the school curriculum. Two computer companies supplied us with software, a number of corporations donated office furniture, and the university provided the space to house the ed tech center," he says.

Krish says they are considering making the center accessible to more parents by offering a busing service. This service would allow parents without cars to attend the courses, increasing participation.

"My best advice is to be flexible in terms of what you offer," says Krish. "Find out what the parents want and need by way of computer education. Try to create courses that parents will enjoy and still support what the [students] are learning in school, but stay away from courses that other adult education programs offer."

For more information about the Education Technology Training Center, contact Bridgeport Public Schools, Bridgeport, CT; telephone (203) 576-7810.

CHAPTER 6

Type 5 Involvement: Decision Making and Governance

To promote type 5 involvement, school leaders should include parents and community residents in school decisions, developing parent leaders and representatives.

Schools have always been locally controlled, but site-based management increases the role of parents and community residents in school governance. This development ensures that schools reflect local priorities and that residents of the community feel ownership and have input to how their tax dollars are allocated in school budgets. A 1988 task force organized by the American Association of School Administrators, the National Association of Elementary School Principals, and the National Association of Secondary School Principals also identified multiple advantages of site-based management.[1] The task force reported that site-based management

- formally recognizes the expertise and competence of those who work in individual schools to make decisions to improve learning
- gives teachers, other staff members, and the community increased input into decisions
- improves morale of teachers
- focuses accountability for decisions
- brings both financial and instructional resources in line with the instructional goals developed in each school
- nurtures and stimulates new leaders at all levels
- increases both the quantity and quality of communication

Some research also indicates that site-based management can improve student achievement. Other research, however, shows no correlation between site-based management and student performance. This chapter focuses on that issue and strategies for optimizing site-based management programs and parent involvement in governance issues.

SITE-BASED STRUCTURE

The specific structure of site-based management varies among districts. According to Peterson,[2] the Akron, Ohio, Central-Hower High School features a nine-member faculty senate in which the principal has only one vote and no veto power. Chicago's local school councils, however, are made up primarily of parents, and they have substantial power, including the ability to hire and fire principals and to approve school budgets and plans.[3]

Most site-based management committees, however, have less influence. They are composed of community residents, parents, school staff members, and school administrators, and the district office maintains authority to recruit, hire, evaluate, discipline, and terminate employment.[4] Guthrie[5] recommends that, in addition to explicitly defined written roles and responsibilities for the school board, superintendent, principal, and site council, each school should produce an annual performance and planning report that identifies how the school is meeting established goals and what it plans for the future. He also suggests that all council members should receive training in decision-making skills, problem solving, conflict resolution, and group dynamics and culture.[6]

EFFECTIVE MANAGEMENT

Effective training is clearly the most important priority if site-based management is to succeed. "Without adequate preparation," writes Peterson-del Mar, "group members are apt to assume familiar authoritarian or passive roles and to think in individualistic rather than corporate terms."[6] Andrew Thomas, community relations coordinator for the Canandaigua City School District in Canandaigua, New York, routinely reviews participation ground rules with all individuals involved in school decisions. Resource 6–1 describes this process. It outlines four basic steps for setting the stage for productive discussion and true accomplishment. Often, says Thomas, the goals envisioned by residents who volunteer for school governance and improvement committees are not met.

Peterson-del Mar also indicates that effective councils have a diverse membership, spanning a wide range of ethnic or racial groups and social classes and that they are most effective when they communicate with other groups. "Parent members can report to parent organizations, teacher members to their departments, and so forth. These liaisons increase people's sense of participation and make for decisions that are more broadly shared."[8]

The Mequon-Theinsville School District in Mequon, Wisconsin, invites parents and community members to participate in curriculum decisions through use of a public forum and a survey (Resource 6–2). Francie Shea, the district's curriculum director, says the survey always provides useful information and that responses to open-ended questions often are the most beneficial part of the survey.

The role of principal in successful site-based management is less that of leader than facilitator. After surveying site councils in Tennessee, Etheridge[9] determined that the most effective principals had a clear vision for the school but were not authoritarian in establishing a course of action. They instead sought input from group members, accepting the fact that their viewpoints would not always be adopted and that others could make sound decisions regarding the school.[10]

DEBATE ON EFFECTIVENESS

Some researchers have concluded that site-based management has no impact on student achievement, dropout rates, attendance, or disciplinary problems. However, they are not prepared to completely dismiss the practice.

Eiseman[10] notes that site-based management improves the overall flow of information when schools are faced with beginning a new program and that it reduces detrimental rumors. These benefits could have residual effects on student achievement simply because stakeholders are acting in concert and have come to consensus on clearly defined goals and roles, which makes overall implementation and instruction smoother. Drury and Levin[11] indicate that the site-based management system contributes to intermediate outcomes that may eventually be reflected in improved student performance. Those outcomes are increased efficiency in the use of resources and personnel, increased professionalism among teachers, curriculum reform, and increased community involvement.

CONCLUSION

Site-based school management councils give parents and community members a voice in school practices and activities, but care is needed in managing them. With too little structure, the group risks being dominated by its most outspoken members. With too much structure, members may not feel that they truly have input to decisions. The appropriate role for the principal is not as leader or dictator but as facilitator—to offer guidance to members and to make sure everyone has a voice.

REFERENCES

1. K. Kubric, School-Based Management, *Educational Resources Information Center Digest*, ED301969 (Eugene, OR: ERIC Clearinghouse on Educational Management, 1988).

2. D. Peterson, School-Based Management and Student Performance, *Educational Resources Information Center Digest*, ED336845 (Eugene, OR: ERIC Clearinghouse on Educational Management, 1991).

3. E.L. Ogletree and E. McHenry, *Chicago Teachers and School Reform* (1990).

4. S.K. Strauber et al., Site-Based Management at Central-Hower, *Educational Leadership* 47, no. 7 (1990): 64–66.

5. J.W. Guthrie, School-Based Management: The Next Needed Education Reform, *Phi Delta Kappan* 68, no. 4 (1986): 305–309.

6. D. Peterson-del Mar, School-Site Councils, *Educational Resources Information Center Digest*, ED369154 (Eugene, OR: ERIC Clearinghouse on Educational Management, 1994): 2.

7. Peterson-del Mar, School-Site Councils: 3.

8. C.P. Etheridge et al., Leadership, Control, Communication and Comprehension: Key Factors in Successful Implementation of SBDM (Paper presented at the Annual Meeting of the Mid-South Educational Research Association, New Orleans, LA, November 1990.)

9. J.W. Eiseman et al., *The Role of Teams in Implementing School Improvement Plans* (Andover, MA: Regional Laboratory for Educational Improvement of the Northeast and Islands, 1989).

10. D. Drury and D. Levin, *School-Based Management: The Changing Locus of Control in American Public Education*. Report prepared for the US Department of Education, Office of Educational Research and Improvement, by Pelavin Associates. February, 1994.

Resource 6–1

Managing Residents on Committees

Andrew Thomas, community relations coordinator for the Canandaigua City School District in Canandaigua, New York, says that his district routinely solicits community opinions about ideas and projects, including a recently constructed long-range plan. More than 100 people were involved in the development process.

Managing different personalities and interests is relatively simple, says Thomas, when project managers follow four guidelines:

1. **Set ground rules and explain what participants can expect to happen**. Whenever members of the public are involved in a school-related decision, Thomas beings by defining terms, including "communication," and outlines school officials' expectations.

   "Communication means that all parties understand each other at all times and that everyone tries to keep everyone informed," he says. "We also stress that understanding is not the same as agreeing. When you have many different people, you can't operate if you're looking for unanimity. You have to strive for consensus. Compromise will be part of that. People must understand that they won't necessarily get everything they ask for and that they shouldn't feel that they're not listened to if that happens. There's a danger for people to take very different stances on an issue and decide that the other side isn't listening."

2. **Make sure participants remain objective**. Individuals who are personally involved with the school in particular ways aren't always effective on committees examining those areas, says

Thomas. Parent volunteers, for example, often are friends of teachers, and therefore should not be on the teacher evaluation committee. "When a situation affects their children, parents tend to focus on that. They're not as effective as when they can look at the whole situation."

As a solution, when district leaders discuss highly charged issues, they group committee participants (e.g., parents or business people), and they listen to how each group perceives an issue. For less divisive topics, participants are split equally among committees, with each committee addressing a different facet of the issue.

3. **Identify goals and time lines for reaching them**. "It's important, too, for everyone to understand exactly what the group should accomplish," says Thomas. Participants often come to the process of believing that this is their chance to reinvent education but later realize that the work is far more difficult and much slower than anticipated. Beginning with agreement on two or three group goals, he says, "eliminates a lot of unrealistic expectations."

4. **Follow the rules of effective meetings**. To maximize community participation, residents must feel they have ample opportunity to contribute to group activities. This, says Thomas, means keeping meetings focused. "A poorly run meeting is easily dominated by one person. Other people feel left out, and eventually they drop out. They stop participating."

Resource 6–2

Using Parent Feedback for Curriculum Decision Making

Francie Shea, Curriculum Director for the Mequon-Thiensville School District, in Mequon, Wisconsin says that her district regularly solicits comments from parents about the quality of the district's curriculum. Shea says, "It's an efficient way to glean information from people."

Before the start of a K–12 curriculum review the school board provides a special meeting for teachers, parents, and interested citizens to share comments, concerns, and ideas about the specific curriculum being revised. These well-attended meetings facilitate the flow of ideas and open the process up to those with an opinion to share about the districts' schools and the curriculum that they teach.

Besides the public hearing on curriculum, the families of every student in the district receive a curriculum questionnaire early in the review process (see "Parent Survey" sample). Ordinarily, a review takes eighteen months from start to finish, and the survey takes place within the first three months. The review committee receives the survey results broken out by item. The open-ended comments section provides some of the most enlightening thoughts and considerations. Shea adds, "We always have room for comments. The comments often are the most beneficial part of the survey!"

The breakout of data by schools can be enlightening for the staff and administration. Michael Dietz, principal at Lake Shore Middle School, believes that feedback from parents and families is essential to improving both the curriculum and its delivery to students. He notes, "It's a way for every parent to have at least an opportunity to contribute to the decision-making process."

The following guidelines are helpful when doing a parent survey on curriculum:

1. **Be clear about the intentions for the survey.** The committee sends a letter explaining the attached survey, the intended use, and instructions for completing it. The district also surveys students and staff at all grade levels as part of the information-gathering process.

2. **Keep the survey brief, but relevant.** When developing a survey, consider items used in previous ones and adapt them if possible. A machine scored format is helpful. Having at least one open-ended comment item provides the opportunity for more extensive comments.

3. **Follow up with random interviews.** After reviewing the comments, Shea recommends interviewing parents at random regarding comments that challenge existing practices, including both the curriculum and pedagogy.

4. **Process the data findings with the curriculum committee.** Both Shea and Dietz believe that devoting committee time to discussing survey findings helps the curriculum review committee to channel its energy productively. These sessions can be lively and unsettling; taking time to listen to feelings of the committee members is important.

5. **Share the results with staff.** There should be no secrets in the use of the data. A "data driven" approach to using parent and family surveys leads to the development of a higher quality curriculum.

Resource 6–2 continued

6. **Use the data.** Commitment to using the data to advance curriculum change is important to everyone involved with the process. Failure to use the data in a meaningful way degrades the entire curriculum review process.

Remember that a flexible approach to type 5 parent involvement can be beneficial. Shea notes that quality curriculum development is an intensive process that requires both com-mitment and professional expertise. Few parents have the time necessary to devote to such an endeavor. Nevertheless, the use of questionnaires, plus open board meetings, special community meetings, and other opportunities for parent feedback provide meaningful ways to engage the entire school community in developing curriculum.

(Courtesy of Dr. Michael Dietz and Francie Shea, Mequon-Thiensville School District, Mequon, Wisconsin)

Mequon-Thiensville School District
Parent Survey, May, 1996

1. Based on your experience during the first five years, rate the overall quality of the science program in the Mequon-Thiensville School District at the **elementary level.**
   a. Excellent
   b. Good to Fair
   c. Poor
   d. Uncertain
   e. Not applicable

2. Based on your experience during the past five years, rate the overall quality of the science program in the Mequon-Thiensville School District at the **middle school level.**
   a. Excellent
   b. Good to Fair
   c. Poor
   d. Uncertain
   e. Not applicable

3. Based on your experience during the past five years, rate the overall quality of the science program in the Mequon-Thiensville School District at the **high school level.**
   a. Excellent
   b. Good to Fair
   c. Poor
   d. Uncertain
   e. Not applicable

4. Based on your experience during the past five years, rate the overall quality of the science program in the Mequon-Thiensville School District.
   a. Excellent
   b. Good to Fair
   c. Poor
   d. Uncertain
   e. Not applicable

5. What is your child's overall attitude toward science as a school subject?
   a. Excellent
   b. Good to Fair
   c. Poor
   d. Uncertain
   e. Not applicable

6. How would you rate the degree of challenge afforded your child in science at your child's present school?
   a. Excellent
   b. Good to Fair
   c. Poor
   d. Uncertain
   e. Not applicable

7. The degree to which my child is presented with new material in science each year.
   a. Excellent
   b. Good to Fair
   c. Poor
   d. Uncertain
   e. Not applicable

8. If your child is experiencing difficulty in science, to what extent are the needs being addressed?

9. Please rate the science texts used in your child's current science class.
   a. Excellent
   b. Good to Fair
   c. Poor
   d. Uncertain
   e. Not applicable

10. Please rate the utilization of computers in the science program.
    a. Excellent
    b. Good to Fair
    c. Poor
    d. Uncertain
    e. Not applicable

11. Please rate the quality of the laboratory equipment in your child's current science class.
    a. Excellent
    b. Good to Fair
    c. Poor
    d. Uncertain
    e. Not applicable

12. Please rate the quality of the laboratory facilities in your child's current class.
    a. Excellent
    b. Good to Fair
    c. Poor
    d. Uncertain
    e. Not applicable

13. Please rate the amount of time given to science instruction in grade K through 8.
    a. Excellent
    b. Good to Fair
    c. Poor
    d. Uncertain
    e. Not applicable

14. Please rate the amount of active learning (e.g., labs, hands-on, problem-solving) activities in science.
    a. Excellent
    b. Good to Fair
    c. Poor
    d. Uncertain
    e. Not applicable

15. Please rate the amount of homework/outside studying for science class.
    a. Excellent
    b. Good to Fair
    c. Poor
    d. Uncertain
    e. Not applicable

16. Please rate the breadth of content of the district science curriculum.
    a. Excellent
    b. Good to Fair
    c. Poor
    d. Uncertain
    e. Not applicable

17. Please rate the quality of teacher instruction in the science curriculum.
    a. Excellent
    b. Good to Fair
    c. Poor
    d. Uncertain
    e. Not applicable

18. Please provide additional comments regarding the strengths and weaknesses of the district's science curriculum.

    _____
    _____
    _____
    _____
    _____
    _____

CHAPTER 7

Type 6 Involvement: Collaborating with the Community

To promote type 6 involvement, school leaders should identify and integrate resources and services from the community to strengthen school programs, family practices, and student learning and development.

To date, research neither supports nor rejects the notion that student performance is improved by school partnerships with businesses, government, social service agencies, and other community groups. But leaders at schools that are part of successful programs say such partnerships are invaluable. "[Solving problems is] much easier when people work together than when they're trying to work alone," says Mercedes Fitzmaurice of Research for Better Schools, in Philadelphia, Pennsylvania.

Like volunteer programs, collaborative partnerships help schools to provide extra programs and services. They also expand school resources and help teachers, counselors, and administrators meet students' ever-changing needs, an especially positive side effect, given the growing number of social responsibilities schools are asked to address. This chapter discusses various aspects of forming and maintaining collaborative relationships with the community.

BENEFITS OF COLLABORATION

The range of benefits that schools reap from collaboration covers a large spectrum, from entire programs and new equipment to occasional classroom speakers. Most benefits, however, can be placed in one of six categories:

1. enhanced academic resources
2. additional programs and services
3. professional expertise and assistance
4. heightened community awareness
5. smoother decision making
6. improved community image and public support

Enhanced Academic Resources

Community Relations Coordinator Andrew Thomas says the public's comfort level in and around school rises when it sees firsthand how schools operate and is invited to use district facilities. "This sometimes leads to greater involvement in classroom volunteer programs," he says.

As an example, Thomas describes a social studies class that was studying the Holocaust. Some community members contacted nearby survivors of the era to speak about their experiences. Because of the community connection, he says, this class was able to participate in a more evocative discussion than if students had only read about the event in their textbooks. "Students were able to hear a firsthand description of what the Holocaust was really like," he says. "The speakers made the horror of the era real, and students began to see what they had read come to life.

They also came to understand the effects that the event had on individuals."

Computer technology is a costly, high-maintenance line item in all school budgets but one that is more manageable thanks to a program set up within the Business–Education Partnership in Eagle County, Colorado (Resource 7–1).

Executive Director Susie Davis says the partnership sponsors a communitywide "Tech Swap," where residents can bring their old computers and accessories to a central location and either donate them to the school or sell them, with a portion of profits going toward a professional growth and development fund for school staff. The net result: the school gets additional computer resources and staff training funds, and residents looking to buy computer equipment have a chance to do so at greatly reduced prices.

Davis says the partnership has sponsored two "Tech Expos." Interest and attendance tripled at the second event. "People held on to equipment that they were no longer using after upgrading, and they donated it to the school. It was obvious that the word was getting out [about the event]," she says. She also believes the events have been partially responsible for a 300 percent increase in district budget money allocated to technology.

Additional Programs and Services

Budget cuts often mean cuts in programs, both academic and extracurricular, and loss of services to students. "The resources given to public schools in New York are decreasing every year," says Principal Blanca Battino, of New York City's Public School 128. "The only option you have as a principal is to seek those resources in other circles."

Through collaboration with community agencies, school districts have found ways to share costs, maintain current programs, and occasionally add valued programs. Two schools and community agencies are doing more with less. A school district is sharing health insurance costs with other government agencies by arranging for group coverage that includes staff members at both organizations, and a school is offering an allied health program to students through cooperation with the local hospital and community college.

Dr. Joan Kowal, former superintendent of the Volusia County Schools in DeLand, Florida, worked with school board members to form Collaborative Connections (Resource 7–2), a partnership of the school district and local government. Through this partnership, the parties have been able to streamline their operations by eliminating duplication of services. They also have been able to reduce costs by sharing health insurance expenses. Rather than both entities maintaining separate group polices, the county and the school district now maintain a joint policy and divide its cost.

Kowal says the agreement is part of the program's push to see the county government and school district in tandem—as a single recipient of tax dollars. "We've saved millions of dollars in the health partnership. It's the [collaboration] we've had to put the most effort into, but it has benefited all taxpayers in the area."

Thanks to a partnership established through the Alliance for Education (Resource 7–3), students in Doylestown, Pennsylvania, have the unique opportunity to receive work experience in a health care setting. Board member Geryl McMullin says students can receive college credit for completing an allied health course offered at the school by the community college. Those who complete the course then work with health care professionals at the hospital. Students have worked in the laboratories at the rehabilitation center and in the X-ray department, and they've seen babies born. The hospital, she says, "has been so supportive that it has given [the school] a room there for teachers to teach on site, so the [students] can spend more time at their facility."

Health care and social services are areas in which collaboration is widely explored by schools. Both Richland County School District One in Columbia, South Carolina, and Paris Public School District in Paris, Arkansas, have been involved in programs to address health issues among students and their families. The School as the Center of the Community Project (Resource 7–4), sponsored by Richland County School District One, focuses on helping families find appropriate health care, and it also provides "seamless service" with various counseling and social service agencies, according to Director Jim Solomon. Solomon is with Columbia College, the lead collaborator and party that secured the project's initial grant money and established the arrangement.

"It's a different way for the agencies to deliver services, and it's a different way for students and parents to access service," he says of the agencies, that each provide one staff member to work at the school with students and their families.

The project has been so successful, in fact, that it is now moving from college control into the hands of the community. And other agencies are taking notice. "There is a growing interest in collaboration among schools and public service agencies [such as] the health department and department of social services," Solomon says. "Our project demonstrated that outstationing of agency personnel in schools was possible and that you could bring together professionals from various agencies and mold them into a team that provides integrated services. It really does promote the school as the center of the community."

In Paris, Arkansas, the Comprehensive School Health Program (Resource 7–5) has been established to improve students' overall health, which affects both their ability to be in school and their focus on learning. Coordinator Anne Sneed says the program uses resources and support from the Arkansas Department of Health and Department of Human Services. The program has eight components: health education, health services, faculty and staff wellness, counseling and social services, physical education, parent and community involvement, nutrition and food services, and promotion of a healthy school environment. This program, she says, has contributed to a rise in ACT scores in recent years.

Sneed is now working with the Mid-South Foundation to secure future funding and to open a health education center, open to the public, on the site of a former health care facility. Two goals of the program are (1) to establish a health information clearinghouse to serve the entire community and (2) to preserve the facility as a health care museum. As part of her proposal, Sneed was asked to show support for the plan from other segments of the community.

"[Foundation representatives] were overwhelmed with the turnout. We had people not only from Paris but also from [neighboring communities] Ozark and Magazine attending, including judges, the mayor, business leaders, law enforcement officials, ministers, health care representatives, parents, and representatives of the Department of Child and Family Services." The district is also collaborating with the state Department of Health to obtain additional health care staff within the district.

Other schools position themselves as clearinghouses for social services, to provide referral options for students who need help beyond that which the school can provide. Individual and Tailored Care (Resource 7–6) is a partnership of the West Valley School District 363 in Spokane, Washington. The program teams schools with social service and counseling agencies to provide wraparound services. Counselors are trained as caseworkers, who can monitor students' care and provide agencies with more in-depth follow-up, as well as empower families to improve their situations. Staff members in each building also serve on a child-study team, which refers students for intervention, says Assistant Superintendent Dr. Sharon H. Mowry.

The program has evolved constantly since it began in 1991. Then, counselors were trained only to provide follow-up support for social service agencies. The intervention staff now focuses on both follow-up and family involvement. "We found that if you don't involve the whole family in creating the intervention plan and decision making [related to it], whatever wonderful ideas you come up with won't happen," she says.

Relationships with agencies and benefits for students in the district continue to grow as a result of the program. "Attendance is improving, behavior is improving in many cases, cooperation with businesses and agencies is improving, and [students] are getting the services that they need. There are very few families in West Valley that have a real need that we don't find some way to meet. We're probably the district recognized most often in this area for collaborating effectively with community agencies to improve family welfare," says Mowry.

The program has also greatly changed the way in which the school district is perceived in the community. "Agencies see us as coordinators for them so that five or six of them don't have to do the same things. We can help filter that out if we sit down together and say, 'Here are

the needs. We can pool our money and expertise more effectively.' We see ourselves that way, and I think they do also, which is very different from where we were five years ago when they saw us as being here just to teach [children] how to read and write."

Principal Battino is also able to provide medical services and social service referrals through Preventive Medicine—a collaborative relationship with neighboring Columbia Presbyterian Medical Center (Resource 7–7). Hospital personnel staff an immunization clinic at the school, where students and their families can receive immunizations, as well as basic checkups. If potential medical problems are detected, additional information and referrals are provided.

Battino says that students are healthier because of the arrangement, and the convenience appeals to families. "Parents in need of medical attention will go into a school building more readily than they'll go to a hospital or clinic. The school is closer and there is less need to take time off work."

Hospital staff members are more aware of the challenges and problems facing students after spending time at the clinic and, as a result, often initiate further involvement. As an example, she cites a physician serving as a mentor who learned that his student's mother wanted to learn English. He organized a group of 12 other medical students and they began a tutoring program in English as a second language. "This was done entirely on their own," says Battino, "as a result of being involved with the student. And it's something we couldn't have afforded otherwise."

Likewise, teachers in Eagle County, Colorado, are better equipped and more willing to incorporate technology into classroom activities, thanks to a low-cost computer purchase program coordinated by the county's Business–Education Partnership (Resource 7–1). Executive Director Davis says the three-way partnership among local banks, computer vendors, and the school district has helped many of the district's teachers purchase home computers at reduced prices and interest rates. To apply for a loan, teachers need only attend a partnership-sponsored vendor exhibition and complete the appropriate paperwork.

Collaboration can also reduce crime, says Michael Simkins, former principal at Baywood Elementary School in Los Osos, California. To prevent vandalism and loitering, Simkins organized the volunteer-led Campus Watch (Resource 7–8) program with the Parent–Teacher Association and the neighborhood surrounding the school. The strategy is a simple but effective means to limit both criminal and accidental damage to school grounds, and it can be implemented at little or no cost.

Project EXCEL is sponsored through a partnership of the school district and the county sheriff's office, the Department of Juvenile Justice, the local police, a community college, the county library services department, and a local gymnasium (Resource 7–9). The program helps students in Sanford, Florida, who've been expelled from school to develop dependable work habits, catch up on lost academic credit, and get back into school. The program serves middle and high school students, and according to Marion Dailey, executive director of instructional and support services, "most EXCEL students leave the program to successfully return to school and receive their diplomas." This program benefits the community because it keeps expelled students off the street and encourages them to return to school, where they can develop the skills needed to become productive residents.

"The parents have been terribly involved because they see [the program] as a saving grace for their children," says Jim Dawson, program supervisor for alternative learning programs and liaison between the school district and Project EXCEL. He also says that cooperation among the agencies involved has improved. The Department of Juvenile Justice, for example, renewed its portion of funding for the program— "a positive sign that they are satisfied with it."

"A lot of resources are coming to the school that haven't been there before," Dawson says. The program recently expanded to additional sites, and now includes a relationship with a not-for-profit treatment facility for juvenile felony offenders. Project EXCEL will provide the educational component of this facility's programs.

Professional Expertise and Assistance

Businesses have expertise and technical know-how that can help school districts operate more smoothly, says Davis, of the Business–Education Partnership. "For example, schools can say to a business, 'We're looking at mediation in upcoming teacher negotiations. Do you have anyone who's been involved with that?' Another example might be schools looking to the business world for strategic planning experience," she says.

One of the programs sponsored by her partnership is a staff education plan, in which computer professionals from businesses volunteer to troubleshoot problems encountered by school staff members. When possible, Davis also arranges for staff computer training sessions.

She believes that business leaders should assist with curriculum development and preparing students for life after graduation. "Shakespeare only goes so far in the working world. Schools have been isolated for so long that they don't always have a picture of what the business world needs. Working side by side with businesses shows schools what they need to concentrate on, and it shows businesses that schools aren't wasting their resources."

Hire Education (Resource 7–10) is a school–business partnership coordinated by the Business, Industry, and Education Alliance in Dover, Delaware. Before the inception of this program, students in area schools perceived little connection between academic performance and their ability to get a job. Shirley O'Connor, executive director of the alliance, says that mindset has been changing since employers began using a fax sheet developed by the alliance to request students' transcripts and attendance records.

"The results have been very encouraging," says O'Connor. The program was endorsed by the National Chamber of Commerce, and organizers are now looking at ways to streamline the program, including the development of a universal transcript form. That, O'Connor says, would make reading transcripts from different districts quicker and easier for business representatives.

Heightened Community Awareness

Just as community outreach can improve the community's knowledge of school activities, it can also improve students' knowledge of what various community agencies offer. The program Teams in Our Community Teaching Our Children (Resource 7–11), at Jefferson Middle School in Jamestown, New York, accomplishes this through regular presentations given by representatives of area nonprofit organizations.

Dr. Thomas J. Mann, principal, says students are more familiar with community resources as a result of the program and that agencies gain much-needed exposure. And he adds that organizations

are more open to working with his schools and that partnerships are more effective when the school and organizations team up.

"In the past it seemed they were afraid to approach schools because everyone did their own thing. Now they know we are receptive and willing to work closely with [groups such as] outside agencies, hospitals, [and] the probation department," he says.

The program has also influenced parents. Their attitudes since the program began have been "more positive," says Mann, and average participation in Parent–Teacher Association meetings is up from four or five individuals to more than 25. Likewise, interest among community organizations has grown. Only a handful of organizations participated in the beginning; now about 28 agencies visit the school to tell students about their missions.

Collaboration can also focus community energy on specific problems. The Educational Summit (Resource 7–12) organized by the Lockport City School District in Lockport, New York, gave the school district, businesses, social service agencies, government, and law enforcement an opportunity to compare notes on what they perceived as pressing youth problems and to discuss ways in which they could cooperatively solve them.

Parent–Teacher Association President Tamre Varallo, who teamed with a school board member to stage the event, says that people who normally don't speak to each other were brought together to discuss problems. Estimated attendance was between 250 and 300. A steering committee brainstormed summit topics for 6 months before deciding to focus on issues related to preschool-age children. At the summit, participants learned about "Parents as Teachers," a program that aims to improve preschoolers' general care and readiness to learn. Small groups discussed how their respective agencies could work together to tackle problematic issues. The initiative has since evolved into an early-childhood Parent–Teacher Association.

"It has made a real impact," says Varallo. The Partners in Pride collaboration with business developed from the first summit and contributed to organization of the second summit. The summit itself helps keep projects focused and provides a forum for discussion.

There is also more openness between the community and the schools. "One of the comments after the first year's summit was that they [businesses] wanted more hands-on access to the schools. They made a lot of comments that there was much they didn't know about schools because it wasn't publicized and that they only heard negative publicity or that they only heard about the schools at budget time. Businesses are also more cooperative [as a result of the collaboration]. If we have a question, they are more open to offering suggestions."

Smoother Decision Making

Governance, planning, and meeting community needs, which many school systems struggle with, is yet another byproduct of working with outside agencies.

The Central Bucks School District in suburban Philadelphia, Pennsylvania, was barely able to keep its head above the waters of rapid growth before it formed the Central Bucks Intergovernmental Cooperative Council (Resource 7–13) with the municipalities inside its boundaries. The council now recognizes the impact of rapid growth on the school district, says board member Jackie Wolchko, and is taking steps to better accommodate growth by using joint data collection and new communication practices. For example,

municipalities now forward information about development planning and zoning ordinances to the school. "That's the kind of information that we need to plan for expanding enrollment. We're getting that communication from them now," she says.

Collaboration also affects how a school system functions, says superintendent Kowal. After implementing several initiatives in the Collaborative Connections program, she says that board members were less likely to take up the kind of pet issues that alienate constituents. Collaboration "forces them to look at the bigger picture," she says. "Because of the standards set by collaboration, there's less acceptance of the 'What's this going to do for my kids' attitude. When members take action, it's in the name of the school board, not because it will be good for the [students] of such-and-such an area."

Improved Community Image and Public Support

Although it certainly is not the foremost goal of community outreach, the public moral and financial support generated when school administrators open their doors to community residents is consistently one reason they do so. "More than 70 percent of taxpayers in our community don't have children in school," says Superintendent Dr. Jon Rednak. "They see their money as being spent on something they don't benefit from. Creating access to schools gives the entire community a feeling of ownership over them. The more people come into the school, the more they're going to know what's going on there, and the more they're going to feel that they're receiving something for their tax dollars."

Community Relations Coordinator Thomas says, "People need to feel ownership in the school because it's an integral part of their community—not just because they're paying taxes to support it." In his community, the school district owns some of the area's best facilities and resources, including a swimming pool, classrooms, audiovisual equipment, an auditorium, even staff expertise. Whenever possible, school officials open the facilities to the public.

Principal Battino believes that support definitely comes from involvement. She says that when people begin referring to a school as theirs, resources and cooperation are easier to obtain. "For us, that bond always brings more money into the school. If [the hospital] receives a grant to provide service to a school, they come to us first."

The end result of this openness often is community support for bond issues and an upward spiral of wealth and growth, says Assistant Superintendent Kleinsmith. "When you vote for bond issues to build schools, you build a better community. If the schools are strong, people want to buy homes there, and property values rise. When the schools lack support, the opposite tends to happen."

Solomon also believes that collaboration builds moral and financial support in the community. Residents in his district recently passed a $180 million bond issue—the largest in state history—for building construction and renovation. Mowry says, "The community sees us as full partners now and [sees] that we can do things that they can't. As far as [collaboration] helping pass levies or bonds, the perception in the community is that we are a caring district and that we do good things for [students] and families. So we have found some wonderful ways to leverage funds."

SCHOOL–BUSINESS PARTNERSHIPS

School–business partnerships are a long-established means of working with the community, and they continue to be fer-

tile ground for improving programs offered by schools.

There are two basic ways to establish a school–business partnership program. The first and perhaps most common is to pair individual businesses and schools through the Chamber of Commerce or a partnership coordinator employed by the district. The school and business in this situation become partners for the school year and work together on specific projects.

A second partnership structure relies on broad-based relationships between the business community and the district. Rather than businesses being arbitrarily assigned to individual schools, they belong to a partnership "network" and agree to make their expertise available to schools as needed. Davis' Business–Education Partnership of Eagle County, Colorado, is a successful example of the second partnership structure. Her program operates through an incorporated not-for-profit organization.

"It was a response to the stop-and-go-and-stop-again nature of the original group," she says. "The first time we tried to organize this body it was as part of a committee. But the committee had no direction and no real leadership, so nothing happened with it. We were finding that school administrators like to meet and philosophize about what the group could accomplish but that business people wanted to actually do something.

"When we started for the second time, we took concrete steps to create a body that would do things. We formed a board, created a mission statement, and incorporated as a not-for-profit organization," says Davis.

Start-up of Partnership

To gain support for the network for the Business–Education Partnership, Davis asked the largest area corporation to hold a meeting for business colleagues to discuss the network's feasibility. Using this company as a project coleader enhanced credibility and participation rates among other firms, she says.

Enlisting support of school administrators was also a top-down process. "We first went to the school board and explained who we were and our mutual interest in education," says Davis. "Then we held a teacher appreciation banquet to plant the seeds for broad support. Business representatives told me they learned a lot about education, and school educators seemed to realize that the business world could be involved in an activity in a completely nonthreatening way."

Businesses that were still interested in the network opportunity were asked to complete questionnaires identifying areas of expertise and services they were willing to provide. That information was compiled in a network member directory, which was distributed to school leaders. Principals, teachers, and other district staff members can call on those resources as needed. This, Davis says, provides administrators with a way to know which businesses are "education friendly," without forcing a school-business relationship on either the school or the private company, as is sometimes the case in traditional "adopt-a-class" arrangements.

Continuous recruiting and publicity efforts are also part of Davis' partnership network. "We do periodic publicity blitzes, and those are followed by a personal contact with business people. I write postcards to individuals we're particularly interested in involving." She also uses postcards to solicit hosts for network breakfasts conducted every 6 weeks to discuss current issues facing the schools.

The Chamber of Commerce has been a key partner in Davis' network success, providing both contacts and credibility. "I put small pieces in the chamber news-letter, which reaches many businesses. The chamber also provided me with a mailing list, which has been a tremendous resource," she says. "Plus, [chamber involvement] seems to improve the network's credibility, which encourages interested businesses to buy in to the organization."

Even when businesses hesitate to make a long-term commitment to schools, there are ways to collaborate that expose students to the working world and business managers and employees to school happenings. Student Professional Growth and Development Day (Resource 7–14) gives all students, elementary through high school, an opportunity to explore various careers by spending the day at a workplace in a career field that interests them. The district arranges with businesses for a student to "shadow" a professional staff member and learn what skills are necessary to be successful in a particular job, says Dr. James H. Van Sciver, superintendent at Lake Forest School District in Felton, Delaware. More than 100 companies participate in the event.

Joan K. Carter, coordinator of volunteer and partnership programs in Volusia County, Florida, says similar programs in her district have "increased public awareness of what our schools are like and what they are attempting to do." In relation to bond issues, she says, businesses have become more aware that they are part of the solution to problems and that they need to support measures that will improve the quality of education.

Making the Connection

Establishing connections with outside agencies is a relatively simple process, says O'Connor, whose Delaware-based Business, Industry, and Education Alliance coordinates projects and partnerships with the Dover school district and area corporations. The best way to begin relationships with businesses and community organizations is for the principals to arrange for introduction to the administrators of those groups. They should not assume that school administrators are known publicly.

"Even in small districts, I've found that business people and educators don't know each other. They live in isolated worlds," says O'Connor.

She began her alliance by organizing a county-wide forum for business leaders and educators to discuss mutual concerns. The specific programs now used in the district grew out of this meeting. Another approach she uses is inviting business leaders to breakfast or lunch to talk about possible projects. For this, O'Connor recommends asking the Chamber of Commerce for assistance. It is a "good resource," she says, because it can provide membership lists and put school leaders in touch with the appropriate business people.

Following initial contacts, school administrators must network their way to success, or at least to a source who can help them with a need or problem, says Rednak. "I find contacts wherever I go. I just ask people if they can lead me to someone who can provide the service I'm looking for."

Battino agrees that personal networking is key to finding collaborative partners. "It's one of the best ways to get established with any institution," she says. "You have to become part of the community and talk about your school [and] your needs and make it known that anyone willing to help will be welcomed and accepted."

One of her most successful partnerships formed as a result of her activity in community groups concerned with public health. "I made contacts and expressed needs. And when the hospital received grant money, [administrators there] knew

me, and [they] knew that I would cooperate, so I was approached to work with them."

Over time, networking and finding potential partners becomes easier, says Rednak. "As you start being successful with the programs and people start reading about them or hearing others talk about them, they start calling to refer you to people they believe may be able to help. The process is about starting a strong, credible program and then reaping the networking benefits as word of its success spreads."

Initially, partnerships may be easiest to establish with organizations having missions that match the school district's or with agencies that share common goals with schools. Former Principal Michael Simkins' California school worked with the local chapter of the Kiwanis Club, of which Simkins is a member, to develop a call-in "story service" for early elementary school-age children. The program is called Learning Is Vital to Education (Resource 7–15).

"The club's emphasis that year was [helping] young children, and it wanted to focus specifically on the age group of birth through five years old," says Simkins. "I chose this as a way to merge the organization's goal with the school's goal of increasing learning opportunities."

Reciprocation

To be successful, school–business partnerships require reciprocation. One of the partnerships arranged by McMullin's Alliance for Education pairs schools with a manufacturer that gives students hands-on instruction about the industry. Teachers, in turn, lead computer courses for the manufacturer's employees. "There is always a two-way street involved," she says. "We teach desktop publishing to an engineering firm's staff, and they teach [students] about working in manufacturing and office environments. This is why our programs work and why employers have been so instrumental in having students there. They need workers."

Davis uses the promise of skilled workers to involve businesses in partnership activities. "We say to businesses, 'We need you because you need us.' What they're getting is a work force that's prepared and ready for the world of work because they've helped prepare students themselves."

However, the promise of a more qualified work force isn't always enough to satisfy businesses, which often donate both money and manpower. They seek return gestures that provide some sort of immediate, tangible benefit to the business, as in McMullin's manufacturing partnership. Other ideas are

- research assistance using school resources or personnel
- student artwork and decorations
- student performances (vocal music, band, dance, or drama) or volunteer service at company events
- access to school recreation and exercise facilities
- free advertising in the school newspaper or newsletter
- student and faculty art assistance in developing promotional and advertising materials

GUIDELINES FROM RESEARCH

Researchers say that patience and clear goals are key elements if a collaborative effort is to be successful. Liontos[1] notes that Melaville[2] stresses the need for a broad shared vision and a practical plan outlining specific objectives and responsibilities if schools are to work successfully with businesses and other community agencies. Other strategies for effective collaboration described by Liontos[3] include

- respect for the procedures and conventions of other partnership participants
- flexibility and compromise
- positive attitude
- willingness to take risks
- an agreement to disagree on specific details, despite a common goal
- persistence
- true desire to change the current method of working together and handling problems

Research also recommends that schools and collaborative partners move slowly and be willing to "wait out" early growing pains. Those in the early stages of collaboration often are eager to create change, says Melaville,[4] but building a strong, trusting relationship with other agencies takes time. In fact, Liontos[5] says that it often takes 1–5 years to get collaborative efforts off the ground and to show positive results.

WORKING WITH LAW ENFORCEMENT AGENCIES

Efforts to maintain student safety and building security have made county and municipal law enforcement officers integral parts of many schools—whether through organized curricula programs such as Drug Abuse Resistance Education (DARE), or because they are based at the school to respond to criminal activity there. Several systems for using law enforcement officers are available to schools.

School Resource Officers

School resource officers are employed and paid by the municipal or county law enforcement agency but are assigned to schools. They are full police officers with full police powers, including the ability to search and arrest. Resource officers may or may not be based at the school itself. Partnerships with school resource officers require constant communication between principals and the officers who are assigned to their schools.

Clearly defined roles and responsibilities for school resource officers and school leaders are also necessary since these officers are held to higher standards of conduct than school personnel. Police officers must act according to police standards. A school administrator, for example, can search a student on the basis of reasonable suspicion that the student possesses contraband. The officer, however, must meet the police standard of "probable cause" before executing the same search. These differences must be clearly determined at the outset of any collaborative partnership to avoid confusion and resentment related to activities that are or are not carried out by officers.

School Police Officers

Unlike school resource officers, school police officers usually work for the school district itself and are managed through a district security and/or law enforcement office. Depending on the limitations of state law, these officers may also have full police powers, including search and arrest.

Private Security Firms

Private firms are sometimes hired by schools that need additional support for school resource officers or school police officers or by schools having problems that do not justify the time or expense associated with full-time officers devoted to campus safety and security. Typically, these individuals lack full police powers. They cannot arrest and they may not be able to search. They can, however, detain students while waiting for administrative intervention. Specific terms must be determined and set out in a contract at the time the school hires the firm.

Benefits

In addition to the added sense of security shared by staff and students, schools benefit in many ways from working with law enforcement officers.

Information on Criminal Trends and Activities

Assistant Principal Dennis Nogiec meets monthly with the chief of police and one or two officers to discuss activities in the community, specific behaviors to watch for in students, and the best ways to respond to them. Sometimes the police provide Nogiec with written information he can distribute to students and parents. "Anything they believe might help parents identify or prevent a problem, they give to me," he says.

Like Nogiec, Assistant Principal Kevin Fillgrove also meets monthly with police officers and more frequently if a situation warrants. "We exchange information that may involve specific students, and we discuss problems. If the police are aware of any type of criminal element moving into the community, they'll warn us of possible problems we may experience," he says. "We also talk about the changing trends and the hot spots. If I find information in school about local crimes, I'll pass that along, too. And if a student is at the center [of a] major situation, the police provide me with information. For example, if a student is selling drugs, it's likely that he or she will try to set up shop on school grounds. The police tip lets us know to watch for signs of activity that violates the school's alcohol and drug policy," he says.

Regular meetings help Fillgrove control the school rumor mill, too. "A teacher or group of students may believe that a specific student was arrested, when in fact he or she hasn't been. Having a direct line to the police department helps me stay informed and dispel rumors before they get out of control."

Training Resources

Nogiec periodically invites officers to advise faculty regarding specific criminal issues affecting schools, such as drug possession, use, and sale. A past meeting featured an officer who explained drug-related jargon used by students and discussed how and where students try to hide drugs at school. The officers also provide staff with information about situations in which the police foresee possible problems, he says.

"When a rock band associated with marijuana and LSD gave a concert nearby, the officer explained how those drugs are distributed and what physical symptoms in students might indicate use," says Nogiec.

Darrell Floyd, principal in Fort Worth, Texas, capitalizes on officers' training expertise. The school's police liaison officer has conducted staff inservice training on various topics, including self-defense, walking safely to a car late at night, and protecting oneself in the general school environment.

Police sometimes are used at training resources beyond the school, as Superintendent and Principal John Metallo points out. To inform students, parents, and the community about police programs and services, high school students in Metallo's district organize Law Nights—once-a-year, informational programs open to the public, which highlight legal and safety issues.

Following a child abduction there several years ago, Metallo arranged for Law Night to focus heavily on preventing a repeat occurrence. "We wanted to give young children the skills to prevent being

involved in an abduction situation, and we showed parents how to deal with the situation. The police department also did free fingerprinting of children," he says.

Deterrents and Confidants

In some school settings, especially where the most serious problems have yet to arise, police visibility at school and school-sponsored events is an effective deterrent to inappropriate student behavior. It also demonstrates to students that police involvement in school is not necessarily limited to lectures, arrests, and other negative events. Nogiec routinely invites police officers to eat lunch in the cafeteria and to attend school events "so students get to know them as something other than a uniform and badge," he says. "Hopefully later, if a student is in trouble or knows someone who is, this familiarity will make it easier for him or her to seek help."

The classroom Adopt-a-Cop program (Resource 7–16) at two Trinidad, Colorado, elementary schools has changed students' perception of law enforcement, says Principal Pat Festi. "We wanted to create a link between law enforcement and children that was friendly and cooperative. We wanted to break the cycle of negativism and bring positive ideas about interaction with law enforcement agencies into students' lives," she says.

Officers from the municipal police force, county sheriff's office, wildlife service, and other area law enforcement agencies volunteer to be "adopted" by a class for the school year. During the year, officers conduct safety programs, lead field trips, teach special skills, and spend time with students.

Law Enforcement

In addition to the less threatening activities of campus police, they also provide law enforcement authority when necessary. Many schools now arrest, issue citations to, and press charges against students when they break the law on school grounds or at school-sponsored activities.

Students who fight typically find themselves in the most trouble. Offenders at Floyd's school face civil charges and a $165 fine, which is "the same penalty that an adult would pay for public assault," he says. The campus liaison officer handles student processing. As part of her zero-tolerance policy, Dorothy Erdman, principal in Eloy, Arizona, calls the police to all fight scenes. In addition, by completing all necessary paperwork to press formal charges, police reinforce the situation's seriousness.

"It sends a message that fighting is serious business. And students are more likely to tell the truth when explaining what happened," she says.

School police or liaison officers also save administrators time by following up on problems like truancy and trespassing, investigating more serious offenses such as theft, and tracking students as they pass through the juvenile justice system. "[School administrators] have many functions. We have a single function," says Stanley Rideout, retired chief of the Department of School Safety in Pittsburgh, Pennsylvania. "They could spend all day doing something that we could do in an hour."

Floyd says that in addition to his on-campus responsibilities of patrolling school grounds, parking lots, restrooms, and hallways and ensuring that visitors have proper identification, his liaison officer visits the homes of truants. "The purpose of the call is to explain the state attendance law. The officer does this after parents refuse to act on the warning letter sent by the school. If the student continues missing school, the officer becomes the school's liaison to the court judge assigned to truancy cases."

Soliciting Cooperation

The extent to which police officers are involved in individual schools varies according to the needs of the school and neighborhood. Large schools with persistent drug problems or gang activity require a stronger police presence than small schools with only occasional incidents.

The responsibility for ensuring the type of relationship needed sits squarely on school administrators' shoulders, says Fillgrove. "Police departments are extremely busy. If you want to build a relationship with them, then you have to go to them and ask for it," he says.

However, asking must be done with care. Wanting too much too soon or not proposing to take on part of the responsibility may cause a backlash against the school. "You have to be completely honest with [law enforcement officers] and tell them what you want to do and how you want to do it," says Fillgrove. "But you have to be understanding and willing to share the burden. If you treat law enforcement as just a service, then that's what you're going to get from it. If you treat officers as experienced professionals with something to offer the schools, they will respond to you. Knowing this difference is important. So many people ask the police to do so many different things that, if you take the wrong approach, a school can be viewed as just another organization asking them to solve its problems."

To maintain an already established relationship with law enforcement, Fillgrove says it's essential for schools to provide two things—reciprocation and recognition.

Reciprocation

Schools must assume some responsibility for making the partnership work and show law enforcement that it is getting something in return for its effort, says Fillgrove. If the initial cooperation doesn't show noticeable results, police enthusiasm will wane.

"Once police feel some ownership in a project, the relationship begins to flow very smoothly," he says. "I've watched police attitudes toward schools change from, 'This is a burden' to 'What else can we do to help?' This change was mostly due to the deterrent factor their involvement had on serious incidents in school. The more involved the police were, the fewer incidents were experienced and the less paperwork police had to file."

Recognition

When police do something to show a presence at school, Fillgrove recognizes it with something tangible but inexpensive—food. "If [officers] have done something for me, or if I just want to keep the school at the front of their minds, I have pizza delivered to the station," he says. "It's not much, but it's a gesture of appreciation that they usually don't get. And it affects their morale regarding school-related assignments," he says.

Some school administrators fear having a police presence in school will hurt the school's image and send a message to students, staff, parents, and the community that the school is unsafe.

The best way to short-circuit this thinking, according to Fillgrove, is to act the same way after involving police that you did before involving them. He says it may take people "a while" to get over any initial shock, but the more police are involved in normal day-to-day activities, the more they are considered just another part of the school, as opposed to being associated with a problem.

RELATIONSHIPS WITH COURT AGENCIES

Social service agencies, juvenile probation officers, and counseling agencies often work with students passing through the court system, making those agencies valuable allies for schools. Fillgrove nurtures an ongoing relationship with the district magistrate who hears all court cases involving charges filed against students.

"[The school administration] invites him annually to meet with us and to discuss new and/or proposed legislation and laws concerning schools, whether they're in the area of attendance or disciplinary areas. He's our advisor on what we can file charges against a student for and what we can't file charges for. He also tells us what will and won't work in a court situation," he says.

Sharing of information about students' criminal activities, both on and off campus, seems to be the greatest benefit of cooperation with court officials, but the privacy restrictions of juvenile court make this illegal in most states. However, school administrators can legally monitor court activity to ensure that students face charges filed against them.

Fillgrove, for example, arranges to have the magistrate contact him when students' cases have passed completely through the system. At the school, Fillgrove keeps a running list of students in the system and what they have been charged with. He crosses names off the list as cases are adjudicated. "The magistrate is more limited in talking about cases than the police are, but he can tell us when a case has been completed. If there's a gap, then I can go back to the police and ask if the paperwork [on the missing case] was completed," he says.

The practice began, Fillgrove says, when the police, school administration, and magistrate, in an effort to deter juvenile crime, agreed to press charges against juveniles when charges are applicable. The information relay helps him see that the agreement is met by all involved.

Court officials also serve as political liaisons, relaying to Fillgrove school-related legislative information. When Pennsylvania investigated revising attendance laws, Fillgrove called the magistrate for information. "He sent me a copy of the proposed legislation and the date it was to be debated," says Fillgrove.

Assistant Principal Joseph Doyle of Levittown, Pennsylvania, routinely works with the court system to process students who receive citations for fighting on school grounds. To avoid disruption of student and staff schedules, however, he asks that the court schedule student hearings after school so students and teachers won't lose class time and so administrators won't be pulled away from school responsibilities.

Doyle attributes this support to the organization of his program and the clarity of his expectations. He offers the following advice for approaching local court officials with a similar collaborative plan:

- *Get the approval of the superintendent and school board.* Discuss the idea with your superintendent before talking with others. Enforcing a policy that includes criminal court cooperation is a serious undertaking. Support of the superintendent and board is a must.
- *Have your goals laid out.* "Clearly state why you want to use this policy, and support your proposal with research," says Doyle. "Know the law. Then show how many students were suspended for fighting, how many injuries there were to students and staff, and any lost teacher time due to fighting."

- *State exactly what you expect from the courts.* "If it's legal to write citations for fighting, you obviously don't have to ask permission to do it. You do need, however, to ask court officials to support your efforts by handing out the stiff penalties. For example, if students receive $25 fines, instead of $100 or $300 fines, your policy will be a joke."

CAUTION IN COLLABORATIVE PROJECTS

Whether working with one social organization or pursuing multiple collaborations with government and other agencies, school administrators should guard against overcommitting themselves. "One of the big challenges of community collaborations is to not get into them so deep that you don't have the resources to handle them correctly," says Thomas. "You must have the means to handle all the balls you're juggling, because if you start dropping them, you're in trouble."

He says the best way to approach collaboration is to take on one small project initially. After they are sure that they are doing "at least a few things right," administrators can move on to larger and/or multiple projects.

Simkins has additional words of warning: Before agreeing to any project with an outside organization, be sure that you believe strongly enough in it to commit to the time and energy its success will require. "The projects you undertake with businesses take time, so you have to make sure that the outcome for students is going to be worth the investment," he says. "While you're spending time on the partnership project, you can't spend time on other school issues. The degree to which my partnerships have succeeded [has] depended upon my initiative to get things going. School administrators must do their part. Without that effort, it's likely that there won't be enough energy devoted to a project to sustain it."

This advice is especially applicable to school–business partnerships, he says. His past affiliations, first with a publisher and then with a retailer, were good reminders that all relationships need balance. The first project—a history of the school published in brochure form—benefited both the school and the students, but Simkins felt that the bulk of the responsibility for the project was his alone. "It didn't seem like a partnership because I was putting all the time into it. In fact, I probably could have done the entire thing without the partner's help," he says. "The experience seemed to be that if I went to the business partner and asked for something, [the business partner] would do it. The business never came to us, however."

Conversely, partnerships in which both parties are committed can yield popular and sizable results, says Davis. Her network for the Business–Education Partnership played key roles in two large-scale school district activities:

1. *Facility construction.* When the high school asked for a special biology laboratory that could be connected to a hydrogrowth laboratory, it also asked that students be involved in the construction process—a request granted by the supervising excavation firm.

   "Students did all the figuring involved in the construction, which was checked by business representatives. The students learned a tremendous amount [about construction and the practical applications of mathematics and science], and the excavation company learned how to teach people," says Davis. "The employer

also improved public relations [and] communication skills and learned what's going on inside schools. The school benefited, obviously, because it received a new lab."

2. *Inservice fund-raising.* A community "Tech Swap" is sending teachers to technology-related inservice training, says Davis. "We ask people to donate their old computer equipment to us and allow us to resell it. Or they can put a price on the equipment themselves. If it sells, they receive 80 percent of the sale price and the partnership receives 20 percent. [The partnership's fund is] used to pay for teachers to attend seminars or conferences about computer use or the Internet. Then they train other staff on the topic."

CONCLUSION

To meet the needs of students and the demands of the community, outreach efforts cannot stop with outreach to parents. Schools simply don't have the resources to meet these needs and demands on their own.

The resources in this chapter clearly show that, when carefully planned and nurtured, partnerships with government, social service agencies, not-for-profit organizations, law enforcement agencies, businesses, and community residents yield capital and human resources in all forms—from classroom speakers, to computers, to the kind of public confidence that leads to support for bond issues. Administrators are wise never to dismiss any suggestion or involvement option. Those who've experienced success say that what seems small in the beginning can become the relationship that defines a school's future.

REFERENCES

1. L.B. Liontos, Building Relationships between Schools and Social Services, *Educational Resources Information Center Digest*, ED33911 (Eugene, OR: ERIC Clearinghouse on Educational Management, 1991).

2. A. Melaville and M.J. Blank, *What It Takes: Structuring Interagency Partnerships To Connect Children and Families with Comprehensive Services* (Washington, DC: Education and Human Resources Consortium, 1991).

3. Liontos, Building Relationships between Schools and Social Services.

4. Melaville and Blank, *What It Takes.*

5. L.B. Liontos, *Social Services and Schools: Building Collaboration That Works*, OSSC bulletin series (Eugene, OR: Oregon School Study Council, November, 1991).

Resource 7–1

Business–Education Technology Partnership

Business–Education Partnership of Eagle County Edwards, Colorado

Issue addressed: Bringing school staff up to speed with computer technology
Agencies involved: School district, area Business–Education Partnership organization, local banks, computer support specialists from businesses, computer manufacturers
Type of community: All areas: countywide population of 22,000
Approximate enrollment: All school districts (less than 10,000)
Start date: 1995

Program Description

It is imperative that students learn to use the technology available to them, but it's difficult to teach them when they know more about computer hardware, software, and the information superhighway than their teachers. The Business–Education Partnership of Eagle County in Edwards, Colorado, is helping area school districts to bring teachers up to speed at home and in school by encouraging them to use computers for research and instructional tools, says Executive Director Susie Davis.

Support in School

Davis says a survey of all school staff told her that technology training was a major need. Teachers often feel silly trying to teach students about computers—something the students generally know more about than they do. The partnership organization—a network of computer support professionals—provides teachers with technical instruction and support for using district computers.

Through public service announcements and newspaper advertisements, Davis recruited volunteer "experts" to answer questions and do troubleshooting on problems. "I also worked with the Chamber of Commerce to put a notice and contact information in its monthly newsletter," she says. "Some businesses agreed to have a technical person available once a week, while others said they would help on an as-needed basis. I followed up with individuals who contacted us directly, as well as with businesses I knew had technical support departments. The volunteers have a variety of skill levels and backgrounds in computers, but they all have enough savvy to sit down with teachers to find where they went wrong and then show them how commands should have been executed."

Support at Home

To make sure that staff members were able to use what they learned at school on a regular basis, Davis arranged a program for special low-interest computer loan or purchase for all school staff members.

The program began with a computer hardware and software display where teachers were able to gather literature on different types of computers and a variety of software. In return for providing the computer dealers a free marketing opportunity, Davis receives discounted prices for school staff members who decide to

Resource 7–1 continued

buy a computer within 3 weeks of the exhibition. "We've done the computer exhibition three times, and [I] have had more than 20 teachers send me order forms each time," she says.

After receiving the order forms, Davis called on another partnership—one with a cooperative of local banks. The partnership was established when the school district agreed to invest money in certificates of deposit held by each bank. In return, the banks offer a computer loan program at only 3 percent interest to the district's staff members.

To apply, staff members submit a personal financial statement about their purchase order form. The banks pay the computer companies, and the school district reimburses the banks. The loans are repaid through staff payroll deductions.

For more information about the Business–Education Partnership, contact Business–Education Partnership of Eagle County, P.O. Box 1384; Edwards, CO 81632; telephone (970) 926-3788.

Resource 7–2

Collaborative Connections

Volusia County School District
DeLand, Florida

Issue addressed: Establishing a way to identify and address mutual concerns of the government and school district, while minimizing duplication of services
Agencies involved: School district, local government agencies
Type of community: Urban
Approximate student enrollment: 58,000
Start date: 1989–1990

Program Description

The Volusia County School District in DeLand, Florida, and Bill Ross, a school board member, established Collaborative Connections with other community agencies to collectively meet the challenges of the rapidly rising demand for services and the rising cost of providing them. These agencies include the county council, 10 chambers of commerce, local colleges and universities, and other government agencies.

According to Joan Kowal, the former superintendent, Ross believed that school districts could learn from each other and from municipal agencies, so he asked if school board members could attend the meetings of other agencies and observe their programs. Initially, this approach helped the organizations to familiarize themselves with specific problems facing all of them and to discuss coping strategies. Now, representatives of the organizations act as a network that meets twice a year to solve problems and discuss current projects, as well as ideas for future collaborations.

Kowal says the program improves communication between the school district and its community. "I wouldn't get very far if I tried to do these things on my own," she says. "But if I explain to another county or municipal administrator that we both work for elected bodies and that those bodies want to demonstrate that they effectively spend tax dollars, he or she sees how working together could be of benefit."

A primary goal of Collaborative Connections is to maximize the use of tax dollars through minimizing duplication of services. "We look for ways to cooperate with each other, identify redundancies, and eliminate them," says Kowal. "We also search for ways to increase government involvement [with district concerns]. First, we recognize the fact that everyone is responsible for effectively using community resources and that resources are limited. Then we talk about overlapping services until we reach a compromise."

Collaborative Projects

In addition to streamlining services, other joint projects have changed the relationship between the school and community.

A school–business "shadowing" program is one example. For 1 day, a business person follows a school employee to learn the demands of his or her job. Then the roles are reversed. Kowal says the experience has improved rapport with businesses and the Chamber of Commerce. "It enhances our image and allows business people to see that school administrators know how to manage effectively."

The partnership also has dissipated rivalry between businesses and schools, and it has shown school administrators what qualities

Resource 7–2 continued

and talents the work force needs. Businesses, for example, don't necessarily want graduates who come with a specific set of skills. They want people ready to learn, who enter the job environment with basic problem-solving and speaking skills.

A health insurance partnership of the district with the county council and community college is another example. "This is a collaboration in which staff at the three agencies receive insurance coverage as part of the same group, under the same provider," she says. The larger group and divided cost mean lower health care expenses for all involved and greater efficiency with tax dollars.

Other collaborative efforts include a parks and recreation program based on intergovernmental agreements that formalize use rights and schedules for city and school recreation facilities, a preschool Head Start program, and student safety programs. A school-impact fee is also added to new home building permits to ease the burden of Volusia County's rapidly growing student population. Fifty percent of the fee is used to fund school expansion and construction.

"It doesn't matter who gets credit for something as long as it gets done," says Kowal. "With this kind of collaboration, we can ask ourselves, 'What can we do to ensure more efficient community services?' The program can only make us stronger."

Sample Materials

The following sections are sample materials used in conjunction with Collaborative Connections.
- A summary of other programs created as a result of Collaborative Connections
- A workshop agenda of issues discussed at a meeting of school and government representatives

For more information about Collaborative Connections, contact Volusia County School District, 200 North Clara Avenue, DeLand, FL 32721; telephone (904) 255-6475.

PROGRAMS RELATED TO COLLABORATIVE CONNECTION

Health Partnership

This is a partnership between Volusia County, the School Board of Volusia County, and Daytona Beach Community College, as a purchasing–management alliance, to take advantage of volume discounts with provider networks and administrative services. It is a health care coalition with the goal to improve the quality of health care, employee health education, and partnering with the medical community. The program is entering its fourth year of operation and has proved to be effective in controlling the costs of health care.

Parks and Recreation Programs

The school board and county council entered into an interlocal agreement in 1990 that formalized an ongoing, cooperative effort involving the use of schools as parks and recreation areas. Currently, the county operates its park and recreational programs at 32 schools, which include open play, league games and practices, and summer, after-school, intersession, and holiday programs. Annual attendance has escalated to more than 175,000 people. Facility usage includes outside play areas and fields, as well as cafeterias and gymnasiums. In return for the use of school facilities, the county makes improvements to the recreational facilities at each school and provides supplemental maintenance services. In collaboration with the county and school principals, the school district coordinates a 5-year capital improvement program.

Opening New Schools

Preparation for a new school begins several years prior to construction. School district and county staff coordinate early during the site-selection process concerning land use and development patterns, environmental constraints, and general infrastructure availability, including roads, utilities, and sidewalks. In the development review process, the school district requests site plan review from various county departments. This is an area where further exploration and coordination is recommended. As attendance area rezoning is anticipated, the two agencies discuss residential development trends and share population data.

Head Start

The county council and the school board are cooperating to provide comprehensive early-childhood development services through the Head Start program. The county provides portable classrooms and comprehensive early-childhood development services to preschool children. The board provides four locations on school board property for the portable classrooms. The county pays the pro rata cost to the school board for supplying utilities, custodial service, and all janitorial supplies. The school district transports and feeds all Head Start enrollees.

School Health

Specific school health services are mandated under federal entitlement and Florida statute. These services are provided by the Volusia County Public Health Unit and Volusia County Schools through cooperative arrangements. Funding comes from a variety of federal, state, and local services. In 1995–1996, each grade school will be staffed by a certified nursing assistant and supervised by a regional community health nurse. Mandatory services include screening for vision, hearing, growth development, and scoliosis. The increased staff will make it possible to assess and arrange appropriate care for on-site injury and acute illness. State funding provides for more intense nurse coverage in high-risk schools and teen-parent programs. In DeLand, hospital taxing district support will expand basic services at West Volusia middle and high schools. Needed nursing supervision of medically compromised children is provided exclusively by the school board through Title I.

Environmental Health

The Volusia County Public Health Unit provides technical assistance to the facilities department in problem solving and communication in environmental health (i.e., indoor air quality and lead in water). The Health Unit is expanding laboratory services for environmental and testing support. The school district contracts with the county for monitoring and testing four domestic supply wells and all waste water treatment plants at area schools.

Food Service

The Volusia County Public Health Unit's Environmental Health Division is required by Florida statute to monitor food services to prevent food-borne illness. This requirement includes the routine inspection of food storage, preparation, and serving to ensure that sanitary hygiene practices are used in the school lunch and breakfast programs. Monitoring of water fountains ensures there are no chemical or bacteriological contaminants.

Communicable Disease

The Volusia County Public Health Unit is required by Florida statute to track the incidence of communicable disease, evaluate this information, and take necessary action to stop or prevent future spread of food-borne, airborne, and water-borne illness and person-to-person transmission. The Volusia County Public Health Unit and Volusia County Schools authorities work closely to intervene and to take corrective action when there are infectious disease threats or outbreaks.

After-School Program

Volusia County Parks and Recreation and the Volusia County Schools' Extended Day Enrichment Program delivers after-school programs at Palm Terrace Elementary and Burns-Oak Hill Elementary. This partnership has allowed us to provide services to students who otherwise could not participate. Cooperative agreements also exist for intersession at Indian River Elementary. The benefits experi-

Resource 7–2 continued

enced by parents and students by having safe, developmentally appropriate after-school activities are an outstanding example of what can be achieved by working together.

Technology: Joint Phones, Maintenance, Geographical Information Services

Through joint bidding, county government, the school district, and the city of DeLand were able to save collectively approximately $130,000 annually for the last 4 years. Further potential cost-saving ventures might include sharing of communication facilities and joint installations such as microwave to transverse the county to replace expensive leased telephone lines. All reasonable sharing of printing services is being accomplished at this time.

Continued collaboration between Geographical Information Services (GIS) and Volusia County Schools through the plotting of maps for presentations and planning purposes increases the efficient response to the challenge of ever-changing geographical configuration, which daily impacts both agencies. New initiatives include possible collaboration in the GIS in Education program sponsored by the software vendor ESRI. Through this program, ESRI supplies GIS software along with world and national data sets to schools at no cost.

The Volusia County School District may want to take advantage of the countywide 800-MHz radio system being used by county government and 14 municipalities in the county. By so doing, the schools would have the ability to communicate with all the governmental elements in the county. The two agencies should explore the placement of antennas on county radio towers to improve the school district's radio coverage.

Transportation

Volusia County Schools provided transportation for Volusia County Parks and Recreation during the summer of 1995, serving 25 recreational facilities, using 38 school buses traveling 67,936 miles.

Emergency Management Services

In accordance with Florida statute, Volusia County Schools, in cooperation with Volusia County Emergency Management and a contractual agreement with the American Red Cross, has specific responsibilities to provide sheltering and transportation services to Volusia County citizens during emergencies. Although all schools may be used as shelters, 33 have been designated as emergency primary shelters during hurricanes. Shelter operations require the cooperative efforts of multiple governmental agencies. Additional collaborative efforts will continue to address facility modifications required for emergency power systems in shelters for people with special medical needs.

Volusia County Schools Student Transportation Services is the lead agency for countywide evacuation transportation during emergencies. This essential responsibility requires coordination among other agencies such as VOTRAN and private nonemergency transportation companies. School district employees have received training and periodically participate in exercises to ensure that these responsibilities can be met efficiently.

Cooperative Business Education

Students enrolled in a business technology program of studies can elect to add an on-the-job training course for credit. This program, Cooperative Business Education, allows students to apply their learning in a real employment situation. Volusia County and the school district have been great supporters of the program by employing students from the school-based courses. After graduation, some of these students have become full-time employees.

New School Planning

Now that the three elementary schools are under construction, coordination is underway on sidewalk construction and the school crossing guard program. The school board's 1995–1996 budget includes the construction of Middle "CC" in Deltona. Site plan review and recreation improvements will be areas addressed by county and school district staff in the coming year. District staff are reviewing sites for Middle "EE" in southeast Volusia and are coordinating its feasibility study with county staff.

Safety

Volusia County Sheriff's Department and the Volusia County School District have supported child safety programs such as crossing guards and school resource officers and work in cooperation with traffic engineering to provide safe walkways, appropriate lighting, and signs and signals for the safety of children.

Health and Human Services Board

Through representation on the Health and Human Services Board, the Volusia County Schools administration participates in providing direction for the local Department of Health and Rehabilitative Services in Volusia and Flagler counties. The Health and Human Services Board identifies priority issues and makes recommendations to the Department of Health Rehabilitative Services and the local community.

WORKSHOP AGENDA

School-to-Work Transition

The Volusia–Flagler Regional School-to-Work Partnership is composed of education, business, industry, employment, and labor representatives. The shared decision-making partnership is working on a planning grant and will be applying for the implementation grant within the next month. The core elements of school-to-work transition are school-based learning, work-based learning, and connecting activities. Once the school-to-work system is developed, students will combine a high-expectation, school-based program with hands-on learning in the workplace. Employers will benefit by finding workers who are prepared for today's demanding jobs. One of our key interests is to develop and expand opportunities for apprenticeship and internship experiences for our students in county government areas.

Health Maintenance Organization

The Health Partnership Plan will explore the possibility of a Request for Proposals for Health Maintenance Organizations, including the possible establishment of a Health Maintenance Organization operated by the Community Choice Health Plan and the Health Partnership Plan. The two agencies will explore collaborative compliance with the January 1, 1997, worker's compensation requirements for establishing a managed health care network. Consideration also should be given to the consolidation of claims administration, purchase of excess insurance, and recovery of funds from the special disability trust fund.

Professional Development Needs

The school board and the county should explore the creation of a bank of instructors to provide teaching services for staff development for the two agencies. In addition, the two agencies will explore ways to offer joint training programs and encourage the mutual purchase of training materials.

Joint Recreational Use at Pine Ridge High School

Pine Ridge High School opened in 1994. After 1 year of operation, district and county staff are exploring the joint use of the recreational areas at Pine Ridge. Three new elementary schools, "P," "S," and "T," were under construction and scheduled to open for school year 1996. Opportunities for recreational joint use were explored at these schools. Additionally, Elementary "N" in Ormond Beach will be under construction soon. Joint use opportunities also will be explored there.

School Television Facilities

The school district, the county, and Daytona Beach Community College will look at the various ways of sharing video production resources, teleconferencing, and interactive television and will continue to explore other technological collaboration.

Resource 7–2 continued

School Board Capital Land Use

During the 1995 legislative session, House Bill 1797 was adopted including amendments to Florida statute 235. The new legislation requires school districts to submit an annual educational facilities report to local government detailing existing educational facilities, their locations, and projected need, as well as the board's capital improvement plan, including planned facilities with funding over the next 3 years and the educational facilities representing the district's unmet need. Florida statute 235.193(7) provides that the district and local government may agree to establish an alternative process for reviewing site plans other than the process described in the statute.

Options for Capital Needs of County and School District

Both the county and the school district should discuss mutual options available over the next several years that would raise the dollars required to support capital needs of both agencies.

Resource 7–3

Alliance for Education

Central Bucks School District
Doylestown, Pennsylvania

Issue addressed: Enhancing communication and relationships between the school district and community organizations
Agencies involved: School district, business and community leaders
Type of community: Suburban
Approximate student enrollment: 13,500
Start date: 1992

Program Description

An ongoing relationship is being built between Central Bucks School District and municipal agencies and businesses within it, thanks to an Alliance for Education formed in 1992. This group of community and business leaders shares information about the southeastern Pennsylvania district, keeps its residents accurately informed of district business and, when possible, develops collaborative projects that share school and community resources. To date, the alliance has played roles in development of the district's strategic plan, creation of a districtwide volunteer program, formation of ongoing school–business partnerships, and accomplishment of changes in systems of information sharing with county agencies. Alliance members have also served on the Chamber of Commerce business and schools committee, which is the district's building committee, says Geryl McMullin, a member of the school board.

McMullin was instrumental in identifying the need for school–community interaction and in organizing and directing the alliance. "The schools worked individually with parent groups," she says. "But we needed something

that would branch out further—something that would provide better channels of communication with the entire community."

Goals and Structure

The alliance is based on the "key communicators" concept, in which school leaders choose high-profile community residents to be ambassadors of school news. "One of our goals [as a school district] is to get information out to alliance members before they can form a negative opinion," says McMullin. "Then it's their job to relay our message to the community."

Members are not limited to a public relations role, however. They're also asked to offer their insight on district-related problems and, when possible, to help develop collaborative programs.

"We wanted to harness the expertise of people by giving them a problem and then asking, 'How do you think we should handle it?' We also wanted to know their feelings about how we were responding to the growth of the student population," says McMullin.

About 35 people throughout the school district and community are currently involved in the alliance. Among them are an accountant, the Parent–Teacher Organization president, the local women's club president, the vocational–technical school director, an attorney, two state representatives, a physician, the county planning commission director, the hospital chief executive officer, a marketing and advertising firm owner, the past president of the Chamber of Commerce, the community col-

Resource 7–3 continued

lege president, and the president of a fund-raising and development corporation.

Projects

The alliance currently is concentrating on the development of more partnerships with the business community, including an arrangement with a local hospital and community college to offer high school students an allied health service course. "The community college would provide an adjunct professor to teach it, and students would receive college credit for completing it," says McMullin.

On completion of the course, students would be placed in a hands-on position at the hospital to learn about health careers. "Students would work side by side with hospital employees in hospital labs, the business office, or the rehabilitation center. Hopefully this will encourage students to enter the allied health profession and earn college credit," she says.

The allied health partnership is being patterned after a successful pilot program that placed students who completed a child development course as staff members in the hospital child-care facility.

McMullin says the alliance is also exploring ways in which non–college-bound students can be apprenticed at businesses, where they can gain practical experience and earn a paycheck at the same time. As an example, she cites working at a car dealership with up-to-date training for auto mechanics.

Academic programs have also been revised, thanks to the alliance. After one member indicated he didn't think that his son had taken enough writing courses before entering college, the district revamped its writing program. "Since then we've integrated writing in all course work at the high school level," says McMullin.

Meetings and Communication

The alliance meets three times a year but may be called together at other times when pressing issues arise. This past year, the group held a special forum to discuss coping strategies related to the rapidly growing community and student population. Members heard presentations from other area municipalities,

businesses, health care representatives, and the county planning commission about their experiences, expectations, and ideas for dealing with explosive increases in the demand for services.

Between meetings, alliance members receive regular updates on district activities, problems, and general information, including enrollment updates, test scores, building and growth reports, board meeting minutes, property purchase reports, and lists of topics of public presentations at board meetings. Packets of topic-specific information including statistics, reports, and research are also compiled and distributed as needed. They typically are related to hot issues.

"The most critical issues are budget related, so we make sure that alliance members have as much budget information as possible and that they understand which specific increases are related to growth in the community," says McMullin. Members also receive information, above and beyond what is reported in the media, about more confidential matters such as teachers' contracts.

McMullin adds that alliance members receive all district publications and that their names are visible in them so residents are informed on whom to speak with if they have questions about the schools.

Organization Process

McMullin initially called on her own personal network of friends and colleagues to generate interest in the alliance. Then she and the district superintendent met individually with each person to explain program goals and what would be expected of members. Community response to the initiative was overwhelmingly positive.

"They were delighted that we made an effort to get them involved. They also expressed that the school district has never reached out to them in the past and viewed this as a very positive step," she says.

Subsequent invitations have been extended via mail and personal meetings.

The creation of jointly sponsored projects has proved to alliance members that it's possible for the community and school district to work together. But, says McMullin, improved communication has been the program's greatest benefit.

The municipal planning commission, for instance, revised its data-reporting methods to provide school officials with growth estimates for the purpose of long-range planning and budgeting for the district. "This is just one example of how the alliance has helped integrate the school district into the community," she says.

Recommendations

For maximum potential for success with this type of program, McMullin says two elements are key: active involvement and a wide range of participants.

Active involvement. Community members who are brought into the alliance must be invested in what's happening, says McMullin. Acting solely as key communicators isn't enough. These volunteers want to feel that they're linked to students.

"Try to get everyone involved in specific projects so they feel that their energy is being used productively," she says. "This also helps alliance members develop a positive attitude toward schools."

A wide range of participants. Public feedback and potential partnerships are limited only by the people invited to participate in the alliance. To be most effective, says McMullin, participants should come from all segments of the community.

She recommends that the following individuals and organizations be invited to participate:

- the newspaper publisher
- the hospital
- the local Chamber of Commerce
- the local or county planning agency
- a physician
- a lawyer
- a representative of a social services agency
- a senior citizen
- a representative of a parent group
- individuals who have consistently been leaders in the business community

The best participants will also possess a specific area of expertise and level of career accomplishment, says McMullin. "These people have a feel for the community."

Sample Materials

The following sections are forms and materials used in conjunction with the Alliance for Education program:

- a description of the alliance
- a summary of core goals of the alliance

For more information about the Alliance for Education, contact Central Bucks School District, 315 West State Street, Doylestown, PA 18901; telephone (215) 345-1400.

ALLIANCE FOR EDUCATION

The Alliance for Education is established to serve in an advisory capacity to the Central Bucks Board of School Directors to enhance positive relationships in and among our schools and community through a commitment to improved communication and the exchange of mutually beneficial experiences.

Why an Alliance?

Central Bucks School District is one of the area's largest employers, with budgets, personnel, and facilities that rival our private sector counterparts. Central Bucks district may accept the opportunity in an active partnership to compare and cooperate with local business and community leaders in discussing various management techniques, procedures, and technology for educational improvement.

Business and community involvement in education is limited only by the resources and creativity available. Effective partnerships review their needs, set priorities, and channel resources into activities that the partners jointly identify.

Goals

The purpose of the alliance is to bring community members, educators, and school board members together to help restructure education to meet the needs of our current students and the students who follow. Questions the alliance will be considering include

Resource 7–3 continued

- How can we best prepare our students for the challenges they will meet in the twenty-first century?
- What are the very best ideas for improving education, creating a more efficient and effective operation, and providing opportunities for greater community involvement?
- How can we provide better communications between the school district and community?
- How can we coordinate the efforts of all groups involved in education?

Composition

The Alliance for Education shall be comprised of both district and community members designated as "key communicators." It is recommended that the alliance be comprised of members who represent the diversity found throughout the community.

District

- Two board members
- Two Central Office administrators
- Two building administrators (one elementary and one secondary)
- Two professional staff (one elementary and one secondary)
- Two support staff
- Administrative assistant for community relations as liaison

Community—one representative from each of the following categories:

- Municipal government
- Chamber of Commerce
- Private corporate business
- Nonprofit corporate business
- Community
- Media
- Parent group
- Consultant
- Marketing/advertising/development
- Social service agency
- Medical doctor
- Retired or senior citizen
- Higher education

- Education foundation liaison
- Former school board member
- Lawyer

Guidelines

It is recommended that the alliance be organized with a standing membership at about 25, with new members being appointed as needed to maintain a group of about 25. The alliance should be organized in such a way that it provides for interest groups or subcommittees in which members can lend their talents in specified areas. The entire alliance should meet a minimum of four times a year, with subcommittees meeting more frequently as needed.

The alliance as a whole and each of the subcommittees are designed to be advisory, with a direct reporting relationship to the Board of School Directors. It is intended that the alliance assist with coordinating many groups currently in operation across the community.

In its advisory role, the Alliance for Education should be responsive to the needs of the elected Board of School Directors. It should also serve as an effective conduit for information between the school district and the community.

Benefits to Central Bucks School District

A genuine alliance is needed for educational improvement. Partnership implies duties and responsibilities on the part of all parties—a cooperative effort. Schools want and need *partners*, not patrons who criticize and dictate.

Joint committees on educational issues allow business, community, and school officials to

- Review current goals
- Design appropriate programs of work
- Provide a forum for discussion of material needs and concerns

Other benefits include activities that bring educational improvement for a limited group of students for a short period. Because such activities are the easiest to accomplish, they should be developed to fit into a long-range plan for overall educational improvement. These activities include

- Field trips
- Resource people in class
- Career days
- Tutoring
- Classes in aspects of business and industry
- Work–study cooperative education programs
- Incentive programs

Benefits to the Community

Although the major emphasis of the alliance is to improve education, there are benefits to the community as well. The school district has many resources that can be shared to meet our community's needs. Many sharing opportunities are discovered when partners apply creativity to the discussion of mutual need and available resources, such as

- Facilities
- Continuing education
- Early-childhood education
- Customized training
- Recreational and fitness programs
- Entertainment

Areas of Opportunity

The Alliance for Education will serve to
- Assess community needs and interests
- Increase both human and material resources to the school district
- Foster school–business partnerships
- Support school district initiatives
- Harness expertise in the community
- Promote volunteerism
- Provide a forum for dialogue and problem solving

Action Ideas

Examples of ideas for action include
- What can we do to better assist students who are not college bound?
- How can we work together to ensure the funding needed for turning priorities into programs?
- How do we make business skills in the community available to the school system? Private sector managers face many of the same personnel, financial, and organizational problems. Cross-fertilization of successful management practices and procedures can result in better business–community–education relations and cost savings for all.

CORE GOALS

Relationships

- Establish positive relationships with the community and build support for the schools
- Establish positive relationships with the press
- Improve communications with citizens who do not have children in school
- Establish positive relationships with community businesses, especially those involved in real estate and construction
- Improve communications and establish partnerships with the municipalities
- Enhance relationships among academic and vocational disciplines
- Establish positive relationships within the district (i.e., student to student and teacher to teacher)
- Establish positive relationships regarding the collective-bargaining process

Resources

- Identify strategies for securing and utilizing community resources
- Utilize teacher feedback to determine need for additional resources
- Expand and institutionalize volunteer program
- Expand school–business partnerships
- Solicit grants from public sources
- Identify alternative funding sources

Redefining and Restructuring of Education

- Establish performance incentives
- Assess quantitative success factors
- Establish apprenticeships
- Expand programs for developing basic life skills
- Investigate year-round school

Resource 7–3 continued

- Develop strategies for parents to complement or extend learning at home
- Expand opportunities for collaboration among students and teachers
- Analyze changes in technology and develop plans for implementation in schools
- Expand opportunities for curriculum integration
- Prepare students for a changing world

Responsiveness to Changes in Community

- Provide independent review of facilities needs and expansion issues
- Identify community's expectations for schools
- Identify economic indicators to use in collective bargaining
- Clarify school's role in dealing with societal issues (e.g., AIDS and values)
- Identify strategies for dealing with negative perception of schools and educators

Resource 7–4

School as the Center of the Community Project

Richland County School District One
Columbia, South Carolina

Issue addressed: Establishing schools as centers of the community, providing educational, social, health, and community services
Agencies involved: School district, local college, South Carolina Departments of Social Services, Mental Health, and Health and Environmental Control
Type of community: Urban
Approximate student enrollment: 27,000
Start date: 1993

Program Description and Goals

When health clinics are too far away and the lines are too long, parents avoid the hassle of finding assistance for their children. This situation, which can lead to health and attention problems in school, was addressed in Columbia, South Carolina, through the School as the Center of the Community Project.

The Richland County School District One project is a crisis-oriented and preventive strategy for addressing the needs of students, their families, and their school communities. The collaboration of health care agencies and a local college, which organized the program, brings quality health care to the children's schools for their own health and their family's. "One of the goals of the program is to promote interprofessional collaboration to provide integrated services at the school site," says the director of the program, Jim Solomon from Columbia College. "We set up a team of professionals, from nurses to social workers to health educators [who] join together to meet not just the basic needs of the students and their families, but all of their health care needs."

Professionals from public service agencies work as a team to build seamless education, health, and social services. Columbia College provided the leadership that brought agencies, the local school district, the participating schools, and their communities into the program.

"Another goal of the program is to promote good health and wellness," says Solomon. As part of the program, each student receives a health screening to find cardiovascular risk factors such as poor nutrition and lack of exercise. "If problems do exist, we will make referrals for physicians the family can visit. If the family is not able to afford a [physician], we do have an advisory committee consisting of physicians, dentists, and nutritionists [who] will provide complimentary services or charge a reduced rate, depending on the patient's need."

"In the three years since the program began, we have seen fewer student suspensions as a result of behavior problems," says Solomon. "The students who need help are now able to receive guidance and counseling right there in their school. We look for even greater results in the years ahead."

Progam Elements

The School as the Center of the Community Project consists of interrelated and complementary components: the One-Stop Shopping

Resource 7–4 continued

Paradigm, professional development, and the Summer Enrichment component.

The One-Stop Shopping Paradigm. "This is the whole concept of offering a number of social [services] and health care services to students and their families all in one place—their school," says Solomon. "The program has built a seamless health and social service process that is easy for members of the school district to use."

Putting together the team of professionals to serve the school district was an organized process. Solomon and the department heads at collaborating agencies worked on together. "I first went to the agencies to discuss the program with the directors so they would buy into the idea. I sent a letter that affirmed our 'contract' for them to provide staff, and the agency directors chose the professionals who would participate in the program."

Solomon says the professionals work under the day-to-day supervision of the school and its principal but are ultimately responsible to supervisors at their respective agencies.

Professional development. "The liberal arts faculty of the college and agency staff join with the school to promote the innovative teaching changes in the curriculum," he says. This includes programs that encourage college students to study in social work and education fields to develop concepts that promote strong, healthy lifestyles. Teachers at the school also incorporate activities that help to strengthen the cardiovascular system, such as exercise and games.

Summer Enrichment. "Every summer we sponsor a session or two that engage students in recreational and educational activities [such as] cultural differences and family histories,"

says Solomon. "The school decides what subject will be the focus of the 2- to 3-week session, and students are encouraged to participate.

"One year the elementary school focused on the cultures of Africa and [learning] how life is different in another country," he says. "We even brought in someone to teach the students a native African dance. The students are excited about the summer programs and many return every year."

Recommendations

Two of the real benefits of the program are the immediate responsiveness to the needs of the children and families and the ability to resolve problems quickly. Another benefit is that teachers and administrators have developed close working relationships with the agency personnel, whose perspectives can be useful in helping the schools to deal with students' behavioral problems.

"However, I caution against expecting immediate change and results," says Solomon. "The team you form with the collaborating agencies is the key to your program. Take your time selecting professionals who will be truly committed to the purpose of the program. Make it clear that they will be functioning as an integrated team, not just performing their jobs as they always have been at their respective agencies.

"Kids and parents don't come with neatly packaged needs," he says. "The key is finding the people you know who can work together and address multiple problems simultaneously."

For more information about the School as the Center of the Community Project, contact Columbia College, 1301 Columbia College Drive, Columbia, SC 29203; telephone (803) 786-3785.

Resource 7–5

Comprehensive School Health Program

Paris Public School District
Paris, Arkansas

Issue addressed: Establishing a model of student wellness and health by setting up the only demonstration site in the state for a major nationwide health initiative
Agencies involved: School district, parents, county health department, neighboring school districts
Type of community: Rural
Approximate student enrollment: 1,300
Start date: 1993

Program Description

Often, absenteeism, truancy, substance abuse, and violence can be resolved through nurturing that some students receive only at school, says Anne Sneed, school health program coordinator for the Paris Public School District in Paris, Arkansas. To that end, Sneed worked with a colleague from a neighboring school district to form the Comprehensive School Health Program. The program focuses on combining the effort of parents, teachers, nurses, counselors, and other professionals to find solutions to student problems.

Agencies involved include the Arkansas Department of Health and Department of Human Services, which locate resources, provide counselors, and handle referrals. "The county and city municipalities also showed their support by funding the new day-care facility built on the Magazine school campus," says Sneed.

The program consists of eight key components: health education, health services, faculty and staff wellness, counseling and social services, physical education, parent and community involvement, nutrition and food services, and healthy school environment.

Two benefits of the Comprehensive School Health Program have been improvement in student awareness of health issues and a subsequent rise in achievement. "Not only do we see students choosing fruit over dessert at lunch time, exercising, and reading the labels on the food they buy, but we've realized an improvement in ACT scores over the past couple of years," Sneed says. "When students feel better about themselves, they are more likely to apply themselves."

Sneed says the primary goals of the program are to encourage healthier lifestyles and to improve the health education curriculum at the school. Teachers from both founding districts, Paris and Magazine, develop different curricula for the schools. For example, teachers met during the summer to compile a notebook full of programs appropriate for different age groups. The notebook can be used as a quick reference for teachers in need of a classroom exercise, such as Nifty Nutrition, which provides sequential learning experiences. By integrating hands-on food experiences with language, art, reading, and mathematics, students in kindergarten through 6th grade learn about nutrition.

"The other goal is to help other districts initiate some, if not all, components into their curriculum," says Sneed. "We serve the area as free consultants regarding the program and

Resource 7–5 continued

offer inservice [training] to other schools and organizations, [such as] the Reading Council."

Interdependent Components

The Comprehensive School Health Program is designed to provide services to the students, parents, community members, and staff of the schools. Since the program begin in 1993, each of the eight components, especially the nutrition and human services elements, have evolved to create a solid base for improving health education and fitness.

Both districts use classroom education, cafeteria environment, and school meal choices to teach students to make healthier food decisions. "Nutrition education programs like Nifty Nutrition and our Health Action Teams integrate hands-on food preparation with language, art, reading, and math skills while teaching nutrition concepts," says Sneed. "Students are urged to try different foods, read the label for nutritional content, and choose healthier snacks and meals."

Healthy lifestyles are encouraged among the faculty and staff so the schools can provide strong role models for the students. If students see teachers and administrators participating in aerobics classes or smoking cessation courses, they are more likely to believe a healthy lifestyle is worth striving for, says Sneed.

The addition of a new facility on the Magazine campus has boosted the day-care aspect of the program. The individuals who work in this capacity care for the preschool children of community members and students and also conduct classes for teen parents and provide young parents the opportunity to experience child care firsthand at the facility.

Keys to Success

"We let the community know about the program through simple brochures, speeches to civic organizations, and [visits] with people one on one," says Sneed. "From the custodians at the schools to the president of our local Chamber of Commerce, everyone is very supportive and that's what makes this program so successful."

Since the program started, other school districts have joined the Paris–Magazine collaboration. Because the school districts in the area are rural, they deal with many of the same problems, which makes it easier to share ideas and help each other find the best way to meet the district's needs.

For more information about the Comprehensive School Health Program, contact Paris Public School District, P.O. Box 645, Paris, AR 72855; telephone (501) 963-6531.

Resource 7–6

Individual and Tailored Care

West Valley School District 363
Spokane, Washington

Issue addressed: Working with social service and government agencies to manage specific student-related cases and to eliminate duplication of services
Agencies involved: School district, social service and government agencies
Type of community: Suburban
Approximate student enrollment: 3,500
Start date: 1991

Program Description and Goals

Many students face problems that require assistance beyond the expertise of schools—alcohol/drug addiction, depression, and poverty, for example. Dr. Sharon H. Mowry, assistant superintendent for instruction at West Valley School District 363 in Spokane, Washington, uses a program called Individual and Tailored Care to fill that void.

The program began with a grant through the University of Washington, evolved from one program into its current form, and has enabled schools to form partnerships with social service and government agencies, develop intervention programs, and improve counselors' professional skills through training about home visitation and family empowerment. Instead of students being assigned an agency caseworker, for example, schools train counselors to serve as case managers to handle student and family referrals and services.

Initially, the program referred students in need to a school child-study team, made up of the school's counselors, to assess a youngster's situation, agree on an intervention strategy such as referral to a social service agency,

complete the appropriate paperwork, and conduct follow-up activities. As a result, school staff had more input regarding agency care of students and were able to provide agencies with more extensive follow-up. Participating agencies benefit because they receive additional clients, and extra casework is handled by school counselors.

The program evolved over time, says Mowry, to include elements of the district's readiness-to-learn program and a much greater degree of family involvement. Now, when intervention is required, the family has input on who is part of the intervention team.

"The team begins assessing a student by saying, 'OK, here's a fourth grader. What would a normal fourth grader be doing?' Then members list the strengths and weaknesses of the particular child and determine how each person can build on the strengths. Each team member takes on a different responsibility, but as the intervention continues, those responsibilities are shifted onto the parents."

The result, she says, has been positive. The carry-over has been especially positive in relation to parent–teacher conferences, because teachers and parents have already brainstormed possible solutions to the student's problems, rather than having to come up with ideas at the time of the conference.

Establishing the Program

To begin, school administrators discussed with counselors the collaboration model and key components of case management—assessment, making a plan, brokering for services,

Resource 7–6 continued

advocacy, and follow-up. They also developed a list of agencies and analyzed the program's strengths and weaknesses. "A portion of the grant money was then used to hire a family service advocate to teach us how to make home visits, interact with agency staff, and gain access to a home with a hostile parent," says Mowry. Paraprofessionals were also hired to serve as counseling assistants.

The counselor team sent letters to 60 agencies, inviting representatives to a presentation about the project. Among those attending were the state department of Child and Family Services, the health department, and the Department of Juvenile Justice. During the meeting, each representative gave a 1-minute summary of the agency's services. Attendees then chose from three options for program involvement.

1. *An advisory team* composed of 12–15 executive-level staff members. This team meets four times a year and is involved in setting goals and providing direction for the program.

2. *A district study team* composed of 20–25 individuals. This team reviews about 10 cases each month. Many cases are referrals from child-study teams—groups at each school that take student case referrals from teachers, counselors, parents, or principals. These cases involve academic, behavioral, or attendance-related problems. Students may be referred to the team if they have attended more than one school so the district can use just one case manager with the family, instead of one for every school.

   "The team structure also helps us cut through red tape," says Mowry. "For example, if a building team is unable to reach the people best suited to help the family, the district team can step in. A child protection service worker serving on the team might personally review the history and make an immediate referral, saving a lot of time and paperwork."

3. *Agencies that put themselves on call* and make their services available to students and families as needed.

Recommendations

Establishing relationships with community service agencies demands clear and consistent communication. Mowry suggests strategies for building strong partnerships.

- *Eliminate jargon from communications.* "When presenting information to parents in either a survey or letter, take out any technical language," says Mowry. "Parents often feel more comfortable with simple, get-to-the-point language."

- *Meet regularly.* When you begin a new partnership, schedule regular meetings throughout the year to talk about how you can help each other.

- *Maintain confidentiality.* "Have parents sign releases before [you take] action regarding their children. Once we gain their confidence, we ask parents what information they would be willing to share with other agencies about their child and his or her situation."

- *Develop a common intake form.* "We've worked with the agencies to develop a common intake form so people have the correct paperwork when they arrive at an agency or are referred from one to another," she says. Be careful when sharing information with other agencies, because confidentiality problems arise when you share information with agencies that have no right to know.

"Four agencies in the consortium developed a computer program that sorts out the information that each agency requires and then prints a form accordingly," says Mowry. "But extra attention must still be given to this subject."

Funding and Public Relations

Although the initial grant—$100,000 a year for 4 years—has expired, Mowry says the district has been able to maintain the program through other sources of funds. The school's consortium with social service and government agencies, as well as the advisory teams and district study teams, put the school system in an excellent position to receive additional funds through the state Family Policy Council and the Washington State Department of Education.

"Representatives from participating agencies have the opportunity to bring handouts about programs and conferences at every advisory meeting," says Mowry. "They also have a chance to explain what's happening at their agencies."

Through the partnership, the school district supports agencies that are applying for grants and provides much-desired public exposure, such as booths at back-to-school events.

For more information about the Individual and Tailored Care program, contact West Valley School District 363, North 2805 Argonne Road, Spokane, WA 99212; telephone (509) 924-2150.

Resource 7–7

Preventive Medicine

Public School 128
New York, New York

Issue addressed: Dealing with lack of immunization among students and families and with problems specific to self-image and self-esteem of inner-city girls
Agencies involved: School, hospital
Type of community: Urban
Approximate student enrollment: 1,455
Start date: 1993

Program Description and Structure

Students at Public School 128 in New York, New York, face problems that principal Blanca Battino cannot handle alone—violence, poverty, broken homes, and drugs. But as a result of her persistence in calling on the community for help, she formed several ongoing partnerships with neighboring Columbia Presbyterian Medical Center that she collectively calls Preventive Medicine.

The program consists of seven projects, all organized in cooperation with various departments at the hospital and funded with hospital research grant money. Individual programs include a literature club, an immunization clinic, a girls sports club, psychiatric nursing services, and preventive tooth care provided by dental students.

Projects

The Girls Literature Club, says Battino, is researching the value of bibliotherapy—the use of books and stories to help students cope with problems. The goal of the program, which is run by the hospital's nursing staff, students, and instructors, is to build girls' self-esteem and sense of purpose through the study of

books about multicultural heroines. Students in the third through fifth grade who participate meet weekly with their grade during lunch recess.

"The nursing department received a grant to build a program tailored to young girls' problem-solving skills," says Battino. "The groups read books and discuss the problems faced by the women in the stories and how they cope with them in spite of the obstacles in their lives." The discussion groups give girls a forum where they can speak out about their fears and concerns. Girls gain confidence through the program, realize that they are not the only ones with problems, and learn about life goals and career options available for women.

The literature club yields academic benefits as well as emotional benefits for participants. "One of the greatest results of that program is the girls' love of books," Battino says, "And the more they read, the better they become at it. We've noticed improvement in the reading scores as a result. And it also helps develop small group interaction skills."

The immunization clinic, staffed by hospital personnel and also paid for with a grant, is located in the school. "We immunize students and their families, as well as distribute health care information, [such as] recommendation of medical specialists or scheduling of appointments for parents," says Battino. "All new students are referred to the clinic, along with the students needing immunization beyond what's documented in their medical records. For the first time, I can say that my school is completely immunized. And it's far less likely that children will get certain diseases that prevent them from being at school and learning things they need to know."

Publicity

To inform parents and the community of the partnership programs at the school, Battino uses fliers, parent workshops, and newsletters. The school also hosts a community awareness day, organized by parents and a substance abuse counselor, to keep the community abreast of programs offered at the school and in the immediate neighborhood.

"Organizations [that] provide services that address the most common problems at our school are invited to display their information and talk to people," she says. "If we hear requests for more information about specific problems, [such as] domestic violence or drug prevention, we particularly encourage the agencies who can help with these problems to participate."

For more information about the Preventive Medicine program, contact Public School 128, 560 West 169th Street, New York, NY 10032; telephone (212) 927-0608.

Resource 7–8

Campus Watch

Baywood Elementary School
Los Osos, California

Issue addressed: Preventing vandalism and developing a sense of responsibility for and ownership of school property among students and their parents
Agencies involved: School, Parent–Teacher Association, neighbors of the school, parents
Type of community: Rural, bedroom community
Approximate student enrollment: 360
Start date: 1993

Program Description

To limit the amount of illicit activity at Baywood Elementary School in Los Osos, California, Michael Simkins, the former principal, organized the Campus Watch program. It's a volunteer-led program that builds a sense of community and shared responsibility for the school by asking students, parents, and neighbors of the school to watch the building and report to the authorities any unusual activity.

Campus Watch successfully accomplishes two things for Simkins' school: It improves the school's relationship with the neighborhood property owners, and it deters vandalism.

Volunteer Organization

"When the program began, one of the volunteer leaders visited homes around the perimeter of the school. She gave all residents a brochure that described the Campus Watch program and asked them to help keep an eye on the school," says Simkins. "The other volunteer leader provides neighbors with updates and makes sure they all know what the program does. If new residents move into the neighborhood, he informs them of the program and of how they can participate.

In addition to neighbors, Campus Watch involves students and parents. Each week a different class is responsible for monitoring activities at the school. On the first day of their watch week, students take home notes reviewing the things parents should do during watch week and the phone numbers to call if they see something out of the ordinary. Teachers receive notices of their class' watch week, and the school newsletter announces which class is on watch duty for the week.

Campus Watch works as a deterrent to vandals, because people don't know when someone will come by. "Each week there are more than 30 students and their parents who know it's their responsibility to keep an eye on the building," says Simkins. "None of the students or parents want to learn that something happened or went unreported during their watch period, so they are careful. Maybe only five or six drive past the school, but before this program existed, no one did."

For more information about Campus Watch, contact Baywood Elementary School, 1330 9th Street, Los Osos, CA 93402; telephone (805) 528-4070, extension 4101.

Resource 7–9

Project EXCEL

Seminole County Public School District
Sanford, Florida

Issue addressed: Providing a nontraditional environment responsive to the educational, psychological, and vocational needs of students who have been expelled from school
Agencies involved: School district, local gymnasium, county sheriff's office, Department of Juvenile Justice, local police department, community college, and county library services
Type of community: Urban
Approximate student enrollment: 54,525
Start date: 1993

Program Description

The School Board of Seminole County in Sanford, Florida, could not sit back and watch expelled students waste their time on the streets while they were away from school, says Marion Dailey, executive director of instructional support services. So the district created Project EXCEL—an alternative education program that gives expelled students a chance to keep up with their studies, gain on-the-job training, and receive counseling that prepares them to return to school.

In collaboration with the Private Industry Council of Seminole County and other business partners, Project EXCEL follows a regular curriculum and is operated like a business. Dailey says that when the program started, a school board member served as the principal of Project EXCEL, with a number of school employees teaching and guiding the students. "The program has expanded at the middle and high school levels, where Private Industry Council is contracted to operate EXCEL as a

separate entity, no longer incorporated with the school board," she says.

The program has worked. "These are the worst of the worst, and most EXCEL students leave the program to successfully return to school and receive their diplomas. It's rewarding to know that the program helped many of these students who would have dropped out of school without EXCEL."

Business Environment

On February 6, 1994, project EXCEL started operating a business simulation model. The concept of the program was simple: All expectations set forth in a business environment would exist within this school.

The model creates an environment for students to be absolutely responsible for their behavior, as defined by professional standards. Part of the work experience these students receive is gained through the operation of a printing department, where they do all the work for printed materials that the school or other outside sources might need.

"Students follow the regular curriculum, including a lot of computerized learning, and catch up on the credits they are missing as a result of their expulsion," says Dailey. After 30 days in the program, students begin to accrue sick days or free days, which they can use as needed. Teachers lead individual and small group instruction, and many students work on a vocational program where part of their instruction includes a regular job in the community.

Like a lot of teenagers, the students in Project EXCEL often have part-time jobs in the com-

Resource 7–9 continued

munity, such as working at a grocery store or restaurant. "The program incorporates their regular job into their learning experience," says Dailey. "The businesses who hire these students work with EXCEL to monitor their attendance, dress, and performance. This teaches the students how important it is to take their work seriously or face the consequences that go along with inappropriate behavior."

Program Goals and Structure

The goal of the program is to meet the educational needs of students who have been expelled, while addressing the behavior that resulted in the expulsion. Students who are expelled from school, whether it be for excessive fighting or other unacceptable behavior, are recommended to the school board for consideration to attend Project EXCEL.

"The school board has the ultimate say about who will or will not be referred to the program," says Dailey. "Rarely are expelled students turned loose into the streets, unless the offense resulting in expulsion was too severe to warrant a second chance, [such as] coming to school with a firearm, for example."

The important element for admission to the program is willingness to participate. Students must show that they are ready to accept the challenge of the program. If they are adamant or apathetic about the assignment, they will not be accepted. Dailey says most students accept the assignment, because they know that their only way back into school is through at least one semester in Project EXCEL, including behavior modification, interaction, and guidance.

Once the students have shown improvement, they go through an interview process to determine whether they are ready to return to school. The progress of students participating in the program is reported regularly between EXCEL leadership and the district school board. The report focuses on attendance, grade point average, and involvement in extracurricular activities or a job.

Cooperation is the key to making a program like this work, says Dailey. By gathering as many people and organizations as possible, Project EXCEL was able to launch an alternative to having expelled students on the street. "The other vital element [is] rules and regulations that meet the needs of the students and serve the mission of the program," she says. "The business setting for EXCEL established professional standards for student behavior and reinforced the idea of professionalism in the 'real world.'"

For more information about Project EXCEL, contact Seminole County Public School District, 1211 Mellonville Avenue, Sanford, FL 32771; telephone (407) 320-0000.

Resource 7–10

Hire Education

The Delaware Business, Industry, and Education Alliance
Dover, Delaware

Issue addressed: Persuading students that their attendance and performance in school directly affect their employment opportunities

Agencies involved: School district, business–education alliance

Type of community: All types

Approximate student enrollment: Open to school districts statewide

Start date: 1995

Program Description and Structure

Many school administrators and teachers motivate students by emphasizing that the better they do in school, the greater their opportunities will be in the world of work. Students, however, don't necessarily perceive this as true, which affects their work ethic, leads to a drop in academic achievement, and, over time, contributes to a decline in the quality of available workers. Superintendent Dr. James H. Van Sciver of the Lake Forest School District in Felton, Delaware, and area colleagues initiated an effort with a statewide business–education alliance to stop this trend by providing fax machines to businesses with which to contact schools about job applicants' past attendance records and grades.

"Most businesses need information right away, and the counselors were concerned about the volume of telephone calls a school may receive [if the program were telephone driven], so the alliance donated enough money to purchase a fax machine for each high school guidance office in the state," says Shirley

O'Connor, director of the Business, Industry, and Education Alliance for Kent and Sussex Counties. Committee members personally delivered the machines to high school counselors.

O'Connor says the program is promising and there has been no resistance from the schools. It has also generated extra publicity through business partners. "For example, the Delaware Association of Builders and Contractors is so excited that it's marketing the program among [its] members," she says.

Educating School Participants

Before launching the Hire Education program in 1995, O'Connor's alliance held a counselor's workshop to ensure that all participants understood the program's goal, how the process worked, and their role in reaching the goal.

"The committee developed a catalogue for participating businesses that lists all high schools with respective contact persons and fax numbers," she says. If a business has a job applicant from a specific high school, it simply looks up the name of the contact person at the applicant's high school, faxes a one-page transcript request form to him or her, and receives pertinent information to use in the hiring decision.

One of the legal concerns the subcommittee faced was the issue of releasing student-related information. Businesses cannot "just ask" for transcripts, for example. "To [obtain] release [of] a transcript, businesses must present

Resource 7–10 continued

the school with a signature of the student applicant 18 years or older. For students younger than 18, a parent signature is required."

Restrictions are also placed on the influence a transcript can have on a business' hiring decision. "Businesses can ask for transcripts as long as they are considered as part of a larger body of information that might include talking with references and a personal interview," says O'Connor.

Promoting Awareness

Promoting awareness of Hire Education is accomplished on two levels: informing businesses of the opportunity and alerting students that businesses would be looking at their records.

O'Connor says the alliance began recruiting companies such as grocery stores, hotels, and fast-food restaurants to participate in the program 10 months before it was launched. This lead time allowed alliance members ample opportunity to promote the program and to allow word of mouth to spread. "Some billboards were created, and alliance members made presentations at Rotary clubs and chambers of commerce. The chambers that have helped recruit for us have brought in more than 200 corporations," she says.

"To inform the students, we developed posters to put at the schools that let them know that these 'performance checks' would be happening," says O'Connor. "We also had representatives of businesses personally go to schools and tell staff and students, 'Yes, this system does work, and students' records and performance do count when they apply for a job.'"

Follow-Up and Future Goals

Although Hire Education is a new program, O'Connor already is planning for the future by developing a uniform transcript for all Delaware high schools.

Monthly follow-up meetings with the subcommittee that developed Hire Education keep O'Connor abreast of what needs to be done to improve the program. "We develop marketing strategies and evaluate the process," she says. Businesses are asked to keep track of how many times per month they contact schools and report contacts to the committee. The committee monitors how many people businesses have hired and how many transcripts have been requested.

"Since the process is new, we also spend time at these meetings talking about problems that arise, [such as] businesses having difficulty reading student transcripts because every high school in Delaware has a different format. Businesses want to look at a paper quickly and know what it says. So we hope to develop a universal format that's very simple and easy to understand."

To get more businesses involved, O'Connor works with chambers of commerce, particularly in the eastern part of the state where the beach area and tourist industry are. These businesses hire many students for summer work, she says.

Sample Materials

On the following pages are documents used in organizing the Hire Education program:
- permission for disclosure of educational records
- one page from the fax catalog listing contact numbers

For more information about the Hire Education program, contact The Delaware Business, Industry, Education Alliance, Robert Short Building, 21 The Green, Dover, DE 19901; telephone (302) 739-4561.

PERMISSION FOR DISCLOSURE OF EDUCATIONAL RECORDS FORM
Please duplicate this form onto your company letterhead.

Fax Number of Company: _____
Please fax this form or mail to above address, attention:

Print name _____ Title _____

Signature _____

Note: When submitted, this authorization will become a part of the student's permanent record in accordance with the Family Rights and Privacy Act of 1974 and P.L. 94-142, Education for All Handicapped Children Act.

Name of student (use legal/maiden, last name): _____

Graduation date: _____

High school presently attending/attended: _____

Permission is granted to disclose the education records listed below:

Cumulative records (i.e., academic grades, attendance data, and group or individually administered test scores)

These records are to be disclosed to only the company indicated above.

The purpose of this disclosure is related to application for employment.

A parent or an eligible student (18 years old) has the legal right to inspect and review education records. Guidelines governing the inspection, review, and amendment of educational records are available through this agency.

Consent means that (1) the parent (or eligible student) has been fully informed of the procedures related to the collection, maintenance, and disclosure of student data in his or her native language or other mode of communication unless it clearly is not feasible to do so; (2) the parent (or eligible student) understands and agrees in writing to the carrying out of the activity and lists the records (if any) that will be released and to whom; and (3) the parent (or eligible student) understands that the granting of consent is voluntary.

I hereby consent to the disclosure of the above records.

Date _____ Signature _____ Print _____
                                                                    (Parent/Guardian/Student 18 years or older)

School/Agency Use Only:

Date this form received: _____ Date data received _____

Signature_____ Print _____

© 1995

Resource 7–10 continued

Sample Page of Contact Numbers

McKean High School   **Telephone**
Larry Cooper   992-5520
Red Clay Consol. School District   Facsimile:
301 McKennan's Church Rd.   992-5528
Wilmington, DE 19808

Middletown High School   **Telephone**
Monica Parker   378-5005
Beverly Heverin, Secretary   Facsimile:
Appoquinimink School District   378-5089
504 S. Broad St.
Middletown, DE 19809

Milford High School   **Telephone:**
Dana Erney   422-1610
Milford School District   Facsimile:
1019 N. Walnut St.   424-5463
Milford, DE 19963-1298

Mt. Pleasant High School   **Telephone:**
James Tosi   762-7125
Brandywine School District   Facsimile:
5201 Washington Blvd.   762-7138
Wilmington, DE 19809

Newark High School   **Telephone:**
Harry Davies   454-2151
Christiana School District   Facsimile:
750 E. Delaware Ave.   454-2218
Newark, DE 19711

Polytech High School   **Telephone:**
Bill Johnston, Guidance Counselor   697-3257
Stan Parker, Career Counselor   Facsimile:
Doris Greene, Secretary   697-4952
Polytech School District
P.O. Box 97
Woodside, DE 19980

Seaford High School   **Telephone:**
Jack Stayton   629-4525
Marsha Dickerson, Secretary   Facsimile:
Seaford School District   629-4527
399 N. Market St.
Seaford, DE 19973

Resource 7–11

Teams in Our Community Teaching Our Children

Jefferson Middle School
Jamestown, New York

Issue addressed: Increasing parent and community involvement in education while informing students about agency programs and services
Agencies involved: Schools, community nonprofit agencies
Type of community: Small city
Approximate student enrollment: 600
Start date: 1992

Program Description and Organization

Effectively incorporating community agencies and organizations in a school means that both staff and students must be aware of what the groups are and what they do. "When I came on board as principal, I asked students about different community organizations—where they were, what they did," says Principal Dr. Thomas J. Mann, at Jefferson Middle School in Jamestown, New York. "The students weren't familiar with them. When I asked students if they knew what the American Red Cross did, for example, their response was, 'Oh, that's where you go to give blood.' So I decided to bring the organizations into the school and introduce them to students."

Mann's resolve resulted in the program Teams in Our Community Teaching Our Children (TIC TOC), which regularly brings nonprofit and community agencies into school to discuss their mission, as well as educational subject matter.

A regular, full-time teacher's aide schedules the visits from local agency representatives, who conduct programs during students' study skills period. The curricula presented vary in length. "Some organizations come in for only one day. Others come in periodically throughout an entire marking period," says Mann. "It really depends on the organization and the amount of time its representatives have. At the school, we're flexible until the program schedule is filled."

Involving Agencies

To test community interest, Mann invited several agency representatives to lunch, where several showed interest in making presentations at the school. To date, more than 15 organizations have participated in the program.

Mann says he hand picks the organizations that become part of the program and prescreens all instructional curricula for age-appropriate content and materials. "I look at the age of our students and how well respected the organizations are in the community," he says. "I have turned down organizations after determining their videotapes and materials were inappropriate for the students."

Presentations have included the area hospital's wellness curriculum, a drug-prevention presentation by the high school chapter of Students Against Doing Drugs, a presentation about rabies by the county health depart-

Resource 7–11 continued

ment, and sessions on personal hygiene and cardiopulmonary resuscitation (CPR).

Community Education Opportunities

A second facet of TIC TOC makes educational programs available to the community. "The school encourages the community to take advantage of courses held at the school. The American Red Cross sponsors a babysitting course, and a teacher's aide who is certified in CPR teaches a class that is open to everyone in the community—students and residents," he says. "We also have an effective parenting program that brings together students [and their parents] to work on communication, relationships, and discipline. The sessions follow a regular curriculum and are open to both students and parents. During the day, however, discussion is more focused on student behavior and parental expectations."

The evening discussion, Mann says, is built around concerns of parents, such as understanding their role and setting expectations for their children. For example, parents work in groups and discuss the problems they are experiencing or have experienced with their children.

Next year, Mann hopes to expand TIC TOC to generate greater senior citizen involvement and to include physical education as part of the wellness program. "Right now we're exploring the idea of a walking or jogging route

with exercise stations that's open to the community," he says.

TIC TOC benefits everyone involved—the students, the community, and the agencies. Mann cites examples.

- *Students.* "They learn about organizations and volunteer opportunities in the community. And some of them become actively involved," he says. "Some students become interested in tutoring or want to participate in the program Youth Engaged in Services—a student volunteer program that involved students in community cleanup and betterment projects."
- *Community.* "The community is happy with the program. Instead of students milling around the plaza, they are out doing things in the community," he says.
- *Agencies.* "We're helping them recruit volunteers, so they're benefiting from the time spent at schools," Mann says. "The program is an effective way for the agencies to spread information about themselves in the community. They come to the school and talk with students, who tell their parents, who in turn tell their friends, acquaintances, and colleagues."

Overall, Mann predicts a bright future for the program. "Last year, programs ran for a semester," he says. "This year, they're a full year long because TIC TOC is growing in popularity."

For more information about TIC TOC, contact Jefferson Middle School, 195 Martin Road, Jamestown, NY 14701; telephone (716) 483-4411.

Resource 7–12

Educational Summit

Lockport City School District
Lockport, New York

Issue addressed: Organizing a system to address youth problems communitywide
Agencies involved: School district, Parent–Teacher Association, community political and business leaders
Type of community: Small town
Approximate student enrollment:
Start date: 1994

Program Description

Politicians have held summit meetings for decades to discuss issues and identify ways to cooperate to improve situations. With this in mind, Robert Pohl, a school board member, and Parent–Teacher Association President Tamre Varallo teamed to stage the Educational Summit that would bridge the gap between school professionals and community experts.

"I've always felt that teachers talk to teachers, superintendents to superintendents, children to children, and businesses to businesses, but they never talk to each other," says Pohl. The Educational Summit provides a forum for all community members who work with children to discuss a specific aspect of education and intervention and to learn how to be more effective in their jobs.

Pohl estimates that between 250 and 300 people in the Lockport City School District in New York participated in the first summit. "In a small city, this is the type of thing that everyone gets involved with, so it was a good mix of people," he says.

Selecting a Topic

Instead of arbitrarily choosing a topic for the summit, Pohl and Varallo applied their belief in collaboration immediately. They organized community focus groups to determine the summit focus. "We sent letters to a cross section of the community—the mayor and town supervisor, teachers, school administrators, parents, business people, and representatives of other community segments. [The letter explained] the educational summit and how we wanted them to participate in a focus group that would choose the summit topic," Pohl explains.

About 2 months before the mailing, however, Varallo made informal telephone calls to key individuals to share the idea. The first meeting was for instructional purposes. "I wanted to stress the need for the community to join together for education," she says. "I also asked each person who attended to choose a representative for a steering committee that would plan the summit."

Group members spent about 6 months brainstorming topic ideas and eventually narrowed its list of 50 to one: preschool issues. This summit topic, says Varallo, would help participants understand the current techniques of early intervention with problem youngsters and how they could be changed or improved to be more effective.

Organizing Summit

After the summit topic was established, Yale University put them in touch with Dr. Robert Henley, a retired superintendent and consultant who was very much involved in the Parents as Teachers program, who agreed to be the summit's keynote speaker.

The planning group covered the costs of staging the summit by soliciting in-kind do-

Resource 7–12 continued

nations. "The PTA and school district put up the balance of the money that was still needed, and registrants were charged $4 for lunch," says Varallo. "Otherwise, we would have spent from $8,000 to $10,000 paying for the keynote speaker, publicity, and other miscellaneous expenses."

Focus group members were assigned specific tasks, such as serving the public relations committee. When it came to publicizing the summit, Pohl says they wanted to do a first-class job to attract as many people as possible. "We talked with a professional advertising agency, and it agreed to help us develop a brochure, which was mailed about two weeks prior to the event. We also advertised through the newspaper and public service announcements on local radio, and we had some favorable editorials in the paper."

Pohl took advantage of one of the three local cable access channels devoted to education, government, and public interest. To add extra clout to the summit, Pohl invited both of his state's US Senators, one of whom attended.

Parents as Teachers Program

Varallo says that, although many things had been tried to increase parent involvement within the district, "nothing seemed to work." To find out what would entice parents to become more involved, Varallo developed a survey for schools to distribute to parents. "We found there was a lot of need in this area. People wanted to know about child development and if their children were on track, for example, as well as activities that would prepare them for school," she says.

Varallo then began researching programs that could meet this need. "We chose 'Parents as Teachers' because program training was available in the area," she says. The program focuses on children from birth through kindergarten. It trains parents to work with other parents on parenting techniques and includes a training booklet and information on how to assess a child's growth and development. These parents go into a home once a month to give other parents literature and to answer their questions. Then the 'teacher parents' come back and meet as a group to talk about their experiences."

Summit Events

The 1-day summit was held at the high school. A brief opening session offered participants a chance to walk through displays of school activities and programs.

"The Key Club at our high school organized the educational displays as part of its curriculum to do community service," says Pohl. Students contacted businesses about exhibiting and asked other schools in the district to develop displays to illustrate an event or program that occurs in their buildings.

"For example, there was an exhibit on geography, and students had to give a presentation," says Pohl. "We also had displays featuring the PTA and a computer business that brought along many of its educational materials."

Dr. Henley made a presentation about the "Parents as Teachers" program and an audience question-and-answer session followed. After a school-prepared lunch, participants divided into groups according to the color of the index card they were given when they arrived.

Each group of approximately 30 people was assigned to discuss a different facet of education. In addition, groups had 1 hour to talk about the principles Henley presented and how they thought they could effectively implement the "Parents as Teachers" program in their respective agencies. The discussion groups then reported their thoughts to the full group, and participants evaluated the summit at its conclusion.

Summit II

A second summit in 1996 focused on technology and involved representatives of the National Aeronautics and Space Administration and the US Department of Education. Varallo says that more than 1,200 people participated in the meeting, where they attended technology sessions sponsored by a variety of organizations, including the Smithsonian Institution and Nynex Corporation.

For more information about the Educational Summit, contact Lockport City School District, 130 Beattie Avenue, Lockport, NY 14094-5099; telephone (716) 439-6435.

Resource 7–13

Central Bucks Intergovernmental Cooperative Council

Central Bucks School District
Doylestown, Pennsylvania

Issue addressed: Dealing with rapid growth in student population and shrinking financial resources
Agencies involved: School district, area city governments
Type of community: Suburban
Approximate student enrollment: 13,500
Start date: 1994

Program Description and Structure

All school and government administrators enjoy growth in their communities, but uncontrolled growth creates more problems than most administrators are prepared to handle, as the Central Bucks School District in Doylestown, Pennsylvania, learned firsthand. Jackie Wolchko, a school board member, says, "All of our schools were at or near capacity. We've added two elementary schools in 12 years, and we're in the process of opening another. We've also expanded all four middle schools and are in the process of expanding the high schools to accommodate another 600 students each."

Wolchko addressed the situation by leading her district and representatives of the local municipalities in forming the Central Bucks Intergovernmental Cooperative Council to develop strategies for coping with burgeoning enrollment. The council is composed of representatives from all municipalities within the school district and school district representatives.

"The real benefit of the cooperative has been that the relationship allows us to coordinate and share information," she says. "For example, we've begun to coordinate data collection. In the past, the municipalities would pass zoning ordinances and development plans, and we at the school district would read about it in the newspaper. There was no way we could prepare for the students who would live in the 165 new homes, because there was no overall plan that required them [municipalities] to notify the school district of their intentions. That's the kind of information that we need to plan for expanding enrollment. We're getting that communication from them now. In fact there's been a significant increase in all communication with municipalities."

Getting Started

To start the program, Wolchko sent a letter describing the municipal–school initiative to area supervisors, township managers, and leaders in the school district. It explained how the district and government share the same tax base and suggested that there could be ways for the two bodies to more effectively use resources.

In response, all nine municipalities sent two or three representatives to an informal meeting to discuss cooperation in local government and the types of things that have been accomplished as a result of cooperation, she

Resource 7–13 continued

says. A speaker on the topic persuaded the group to form a steering committee, which included Wolchko, to determine the council's structure and to identify areas of mutual concern.

"We developed a purpose, goals, representation, objectives, and areas of collaboration for the cooperative, [such as] sharing facilities, cooperating on legislation, and working together on administrative functions." Representatives of each municipality then took the proposed structure back to their respective boards for review and to pass a resolution joining the cooperative.

Meeting Topics

Each council meeting is devoted to a single topic. Wolchko says the first meeting revealed everyone's concern about the area's rapid growth. "One of the first things we did was put together a panel of experts to discuss growth and its effects. We invited people from the Greenspace Alliance, a local landscape architect, a community planner, and various representatives of the different segments of the community that could provide some expertise in how to manage rapid growth," she says.

Explaining the invisible economics of real estate development and the loss of open space, the panel reviewed a formula that illustrated the costs of development versus the costs of expanding school and community resources. According to Wolchko, members learned that there was a shortfall of $4,700 per new student, which raised awareness of the costs of development. "Two of the municipalities have since put forth referendums to raise tax dollars to buy the development rights to land," she says. "They want to preserve the open space as park or wildlife areas rather than [having to] spend money [later] developing the land for schools and services the community needs."

Subsequent council meetings have focused on various issues, including recreation. "The municipalities provide fields for soccer, as does each school. The meeting prompted a discussion on how the school district, through its community relations office, could jointly manage these properties. With the municipal athletic associations, the district could develop a master plan for field use and availability," says Wolchko.

Potential Problems

Establishing a cooperative is not without problems, according to Wolchko. "Personalities are a key factor. Some municipalities continue to protect their municipal boundaries and don't adopt the regional approach."

She says a cooperative may be especially prone to this policy when faced with a serious decision. "When a cooperative member votes against a resolution, it's likely that his or her municipality also supports that position, and that can spill over into the intergovernmental cooperative. We've had occasions when a municipality has withdrawn from the council because of a single issue, so it's important to recognize that this type of feeling can eat away at any cooperative effort."

Sample Matierals

On the following pages are materials that have been used by the Central Bucks Intergovernmental Cooperative Council:
- the charter recommended by a steering committee that formed the organization
- the committee resolution resulting from the meeting

Wolchko recommends that administrators interested in beginning an intergovernmental cooperative council read a State of Pennsylvania publication, *Intergovernmental Cooperation Handbook*. She calls it the "bible" of cooperation. To inquire about receiving a copy, call The Pennsylvania Bureau of Publications, Pennsylvania Department of General Services, (717) 787-3273.

For more information about the Intergovernmental Cooperative Council, contact Central Bucks School District, 315 West State Street, Doylestown, PA 18901; telephone (215) 345-1400.

CHARTER

Steering Committee Recommendation: Formation of a municipal–school district cooperative to be named—

Central Bucks
Intergovernmental Cooperative Council

Purpose: Provide an organized structure to bring locally elected and appointed officials of the Central Bucks School District and its municipalities into a collaborative framework to exchange information and ideas to promote cooperation.

Goal: Identify areas of mutual concern whereby the existing resources of a common tax base might be better or more efficiently utilized.

Representation: Advisory council to consist of a representative of each of the participating municipalities plus one alternate from each and two school board representatives plus one alternate.

Procedure: Matters brought before the council will be decided by majority vote. Each municipality with membership on the council will have one vote. The school district will have two votes. Action of the advisory council will require ratification by a majority of the member bodies.

Objectives: Foster cooperation between government agencies.
Develop a plan for growth management in Central Bucks.
Coordinate strategies for development of cooperative agreements.

Areas of
Cooperation: Growth management—Planning and development
Shared facilities
• Public buildings
• Open space/recreational areas
Shared activities
• Maintenance of public properties
• Joint purchasing
• Equipment and supplies
• Service contracts
Legislative action
Administrative functions
• Information
• Data collection/exchange
• Comprehensive studies
• Communication

Authority: Intergovernmental Cooperation Act of 1972

Resource 7–13 continued

Resolution
of
Central Bucks Intergovernmental Cooperative Council

No: 0001

Date: June 15, 1995

Whereas

the Central Bucks Intergovernmental Cooperative Council consists of representatives from the nine Central Bucks municipalities and the Central Bucks School District.

Whereas

the Central Bucks Intergovernmental Cooperative Council has actively pursued farmland and open space preservation. The Central Bucks Intergovernmental Cooperative Council held a forum and sought public input on possible ways to preserve the dwindling farmland and open space in Bucks County at several of its public meetings.

Whereas

the Central Bucks Intergovernmental Cooperative Council believes that the greatest opportunity for success in preserving farmland and open space exists at the level of country government.

Now, therefore be it resolved

that the Central Bucks Intergovernmental Cooperative recommends and encourages the Commissioners of the County of Bucks to create a Farmland and Open Space Task Force to function at the county level.

Further resolved,

the Central Bucks Intergovernmental Cooperative Council recommends and encourages the county commissioners to staff this task force with equal representation from all parts of the county.

Adopted this 15th day of June 1995

—Representative, Buckingham Township
—Representative, Central Bucks School District
—Representative, Central Bucks School District
—Representative, Doylestown Borough
—Representative, Doylestown Township
—Representative, New Britain Borough
—Representative, New Britain Township
—Representative, Plumstead Township
—Representative, Warrington Township
—Representative, Warwick Township

HONORARY MEMBERS

State Representatives
US Senators

ATTEST:

_____

Secretary

Resource 7–14

Student Professional Growth and Development Day

Lake Forest School District
Felton, Delaware

Issue addressed: Helping students make the transition from school to work by exposing them to careers and the skills necessary to be successful in them

Agencies involved: School district, parents, businesses

Type of community: Rural, bedroom community

Approximate student enrollment: 3,500

Start date: 1992

Program Description and Structure

To persuade students that what they learn in school will affect them later in life, staff members at Lake Forest School District in Felton, Delaware, took students directly to the most reliable source of career information—professionals already in the field.

Led by staff member Karen Garrison and Dr. James H. Van Sciver, superintendent, the district organized a Professional Growth and Development Day for all students from first through twelfth grades. The purpose was to teach students exactly which skills they will need to be successful in career fields of interest to them. The premise of the event is simple: Students had the option to choose an occupation they would like to observe. They were then assigned to a professional in that field and allowed to "shadow" that person for a full workday.

"It gave students an opportunity to experience what it would be like to be a dentist or politician or company manager. They could talk with a vice-president of marketing or personnel director about the job and the skills necessary to be successful," says Van Sciver. "And it also helped the school district develop strong bonds with businesses."

Students were responsible for their own transportation to the businesses where they were assigned. "Some were able to ride to work with their parents, and some were placed at sites where they could walk," he continues. "More than 100 companies participated in the program, so all 3,500 students in the system had a successful day interacting in the workplace or talking with people about the importance of things like attendance."

Organization Process

Van Sciver credits his administrative assistant with bringing the idea to fruition. "She contacted numerous businesses in both the private and public sectors, including the governor's office, the lieutenant governor's office, and industries in the immediate area and described her goal: to provide students who want to participate in some shadowing experience."

From that point, an advisory committee of parents, school counselors, representatives from the business and education alliance, and business people was formed to help plan, implement, and analyze evaluation results of the program. The entire planning process took about 1 year.

Courtesy of Lake Forest School District, Felton, Delaware.

Resource 7–14 continued

Students were placed at businesses according to their interests. The committee contacted businesses to ask for their cooperation and then made a list of the opportunities available. Students then signed up according to their preference. "We strongly encouraged parents to take students to work with them," says Van Sciver.

Students who chose not to participate in the shadowing experience were involved in career-oriented activities at their respective schools.

At the elementary schools, 15 different people, including a dentist and representatives from Dover Air Force Base, gave presentations about their career fields and set up tables where students could learn more about them. Career fairs were staged at the middle school and high school. "We wanted to have an experience prepared for the students who didn't want to go to businesses for the day," Van Sciver says. "This was a good way to provide them with similar information."

Teacher Activities

Van Sciver says classroom teachers used the event as a catalyst for classroom activities. "In a lot of cases, teachers used the shadowing day as a chance to reinforce students' writing skills. For example, they would have students write to the employers thanking them for the experience and describing what they learned from it."

Teachers also helped prepare students for their trips into the business world by explaining the importance of dressing for the job. "They stressed that every job has a type of uniform. If a student was going to shadow a vice-president of a company, then the student should look like he or she belonged," explains Van Sciver.

The preparatory efforts did not go unnoticed. "One of the things the employers said many times was that the students were well dressed, respectful, and eager about where they had been placed," says Van Sciver.

Planning Recommendations

Van Sciver has the following advice for other administrators who may be interested in conducting a similar event on a districtwide scale:

Take the time to do it right. "If you do something, be sure that you do it well," he says. "There is nothing worse than inviting the private sector into your building and then not having them enjoy the experience."

"It's very important to make the event a positive community relations experience. That means making sure everything goes smoothly by investing time to ensure that schedules are organized and [that] you have a backup plan if someone is ill or the unexpected happens," he says. "For example, we had two high school girls who were scheduled to go somewhere to shadow staff members, and they didn't go. So we had the girls write letters to the companies explaining their absences."

Stress to students the image they project. "The way students handle themselves can make an event like this easier or more difficult for the school district," says Van Sciver. "We make sure students understand that when they are at a place of business, they are not just representing themselves. They are also representing their families, the school, and the district."

Be prepared for criticism from staff. "Whenever you use instructional time for a nonacademic activity, staff will criticize you, and it's no different in this situation," he says. "It's important to sell staff members on this, however, because if they don't believe in what you're doing, they'll project that to students. Then students won't take it seriously either.

"We stressed to staff members that it was important for students to see the connection between work and school," he continues. "If students see how the things they learn in school are used in work, they will be more inclined to put forth an effort toward their studies and attendance."

For more information about the Student Professional Growth and Development Day, contact Lake Forest School District, 5423 Killens Pond Road, Felton, DE 19943; telephone (302) 284-3020.

Resource 7–15

Learning Is Vital to Education

Baywood Elementary School
Los Osos, California

Issue addressed: Improving community and student literacy
Agencies involved: School, community literacy council
Type of community: Rural, bedroom community
Approximate student enrollment: 360
Start date: 1995

Program Description

School effectiveness has been measured by reading comprehension for years—the higher the level of student reading, the better the school. Changing student populations, however, are challenging schools to be more effective than ever in this area. Prompted by the many children who grow up in homes where English is a second language or a single parent doesn't have time to read with them, Michael Simkins, former principal of Baywood Elementary School in Los Osos, California, launched a tutoring program suggested by a parent. This program, which helps students to improve their reading skills, operates through a partnership with the area literacy council.

The goal of the tutoring program is simply to increase the reading proficiency of students struggling to keep up with their peers. Simkins explains that reading tutors are available at his school but only through a special program that helps first graders learn to read.

"If we have new students in the district who have trouble reading or second graders who have problems keeping up, there aren't opportunities for them to receive any outside help," he says.

To solve this problem, Simkins started looking at minigrants offered by a local utility company to aid at-risk students. Meanwhile, a parent involved with the literacy council proposed that the school could provide a location for training volunteers to work with students. And the council agreed to jointly apply for a minigrant.

Implementation

After receiving the grant, the school and literacy council publicized the plan and solicited individuals to volunteer as tutors. Solicitations explaining tutor training were circulated through newspapers, television, and letters sent home with students. The bulk of participants are parents, but anyone interested in the program can join, including other students.

"We encouraged both adults and older elementary students to take the 50-hour training program conducted by the literacy council," says Simkins. A few fifth and sixth grade students volunteered for the program and will be used with the beginning-level readers. The training—two hours per night, five nights a week for five weeks—taught volunteers the essence of how people learn to read and how to effectively teach the students to improve their reading skills.

While volunteers received their tutor training, Simkins asked teachers to recommend children needing the most help. Once teachers referred students with reading problems to the program, Simkins followed up with a per-

Resource 7–15 continued

mission letter to the parents, explaining the program and asking for a signature.

"Occasionally, students with reading problems have parents who cannot read and therefore don't understand the letter," says Simkins. "When permission forms don't get returned, I call the parents to ensure they understand the benefit of the program."

Students enrolled in the program are matched with one of 22 trained tutors and receive 30–40 minutes of help after school is dismissed. Tutoring sessions are typically held at the school, but parents do have the option of arranging for tutors to work with their children at their homes. Simkins discourages this, however, because tutors are volunteers and don't necessarily come with the stamp of "golden moral character" that teachers have. "At school the tutors are in an open room with other people, so they are never alone in a room with a student," he says.

For more information about the Learning Is Vital to Education program, contact Baywood Elementary School, 1330 9th Street, Los Osos, CA 93402; telephone (805) 528-4070, extension 4101.

Resource 7–16

Classroom Adopt-a-Cop

Eckhart Elementary School and East Street School
Trinidad, Colorado

Issue addressed: Changing students' negative perception of law enforcement officers
Agencies involved: School, local police department, highway patrol, Colorado Division of Wildlife
Type of community: Small city
Start date: 1993

Program Description and Goals

Although school administrators, teachers, and staff members repeatedly tell students that law enforcement agencies exist to help them, it is difficult to persuade students that this is true, especially if their experiences with law enforcement have been negative.

An Adopt-a-Cop program started by Principal Pat Festi at Eckhart Primary School and East Street School in Trinidad, Colorado, invites police and other law enforcement officers to volunteer their free time to help create positive perceptions of law enforcement among students. "The police chief and I both felt that, in the community, most contact between the police and students' parents came about because of negative things," says Festi. "We wanted to create a link between law enforcement and children that was friendly and cooperative—something that would break the cycle of negativism and bring positive ideas about interaction with law enforcement agencies into students' lives."

The Adopt-a-Cop program has three primary goals:

1. to provide rewarding activities for the students

2. to educate students about crime prevention and safety

3. to provide students with the skills necessary to resist using or otherwise becoming involved with drugs and alcohol

"The program has generated positive thinking among students that law enforcement officials are not present only in times of danger. They're around all the time," says Festi. "Officials tell me that their school visits are a very positive part of their day. Most of the time they're dealing with problems and other negative issues," says Festi. "But volunteering in the schools is a real morale builder for them."

Adoption and Activities

Officers interested in volunteering at the school during their days off ask their supervisors to prepare a "Wanted" poster featuring a picture of the officer and a brief summary of his or her background and interests. Festi distributes the posters among the classes, and the students choose which officer from the police department, highway patrol, or state Division of Wildlife they would like to adopt.

"After adoptions are complete, I keep in close contact with the police chief and other agency heads to talk about what officers have planned," she says. "If an officer can't make it to school at his or her designated time, he or she will usually call me to reschedule a time."

Volunteer officers conduct activities in and outside the schools. Most activities incorporate an element of safety education, such as fingerprinting, safety in school, fire preven-

Resource 7–16 continued

tion, first aid, cardiopulmonary resuscitation, or crime prevention. They've also done specific age-related programs about Halloween safety, bicycle safety, and strangers.

"Officers come to school to participate in classroom lunch, physical education periods, [and] playground activities and sometimes lead their classes on field trips," says Festi. "For example, they've taken students to the courthouse, the police department, and other agencies to show students what their job is all about and how the agencies work."

Officers' personal interests have also been topics of classroom presentations. "If officers have an area of expertise such as a musical instrument, dog grooming, calligraphy, or any other hobbies, they may do that as a program."

Some officers even take students to community events. "They've been very good about buying extra tickets and taking children if something comes through town. These are mostly sports events, [such as] the Harlem Globetrotters, but there may also be a circus," she says.

Results

Festi says the program made a lasting impression on a student who moved out of town.

"One of our children moved to another city after last year and knew he should call for help one night when his mother didn't come home," she says. "He called us here at the school."

"He told me he called the school because he knew that I would be able to send someone to help him. When I asked him how he knew that, his response was, 'Because you had our cops in school, and they said they would always be here to help us.' The program obviously carried over as a positive thing in this child's life."

For more information about the Adopt-a-Cop program, contact Eckhart Elementary School, 1021 Pierce Street, Trinidad, CO 81082, telephone (719) 846-2122, or East Street School, 206 East Street, Trinidad, CO 81082, telephone (719) 846-6995.

Index